ARCADE
PUBLICATIONS

Constructing the Flinders Street viaduct, c. 1890

Making MODERN MELBOURNE

JENNY LEE

Published by Arcade Publications
PO Box 1189
Carlton VIC 3053 Australia

National Library of Australia Cataloguing-in-Publication entry:

Lee, Jenny, 1953-
Making Modern Melbourne / Jenny Lee.

ISBN 9780980436716 (pbk.)

Bibliography. Melbourne (Vic.)–History.

994.51

Designed by Peter Daniel
Contemporary photography by Holly Campbell
Printed by Griffin Press
Distributed by Dennis Jones & Associates

Images on pp. ii–iii, 2–3, 11, 20–21, 29, 30–31, 34, 36–37, 40,
49, 51, 52–53, 55, 57, 59 (top), 60–61, 68, 69 (top), 70 (top),
71 (top), 74 (top), 77, 82, 87, 89, 92, 93, 94, 95, 105, 107, 108,
114, 121 (top), 125, 134 (top) and 138–39 from the Pictures
Collection of the State Library of Victoria. Courtesy of the State
Library of Victoria.

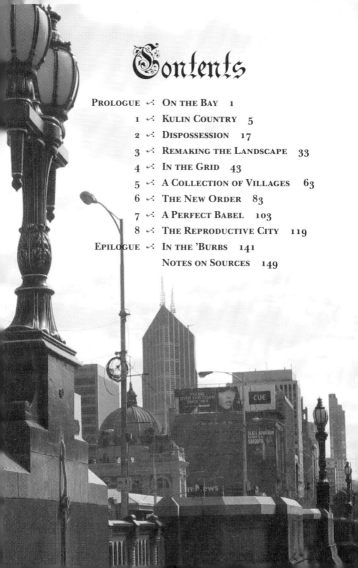

Contents

PROLOGUE ⌣ ON THE BAY   1

1 ⌣ KULIN COUNTRY   5

2 ⌣ DISPOSSESSION   17

3 ⌣ REMAKING THE LANDSCAPE   33

4 ⌣ IN THE GRID   43

5 ⌣ A COLLECTION OF VILLAGES   63

6 ⌣ THE NEW ORDER   83

7 ⌣ A PERFECT BABEL   103

8 ⌣ THE REPRODUCTIVE CITY   119

EPILOGUE ⌣ IN THE 'BURBS   141

NOTES ON SOURCES   149

Photo by Viv Mehes 1995
From the series 'The River Mouth' in the exhibition
'Big River – Soundings on the Lower Yarra'
122 cm x 122 cm silver gelatin print

ON THE BAY

It's a clear autumn day, and a steady wind has blown away the city smog. Far from shore, out on Port Phillip Bay, I lean over the side of the boat to smell the sea tang. Below me, garfish flash silver; occasionally a larger shape probes upwards, then dives as we approach. Seabirds bob in our wake, looking for an easy feed. The water is clear – blue-green and deep, but not ocean-deep.

I know it's not always like this. The bay is notorious for sudden storms and treacherous currents. In the Rip at its mouth, the tide runs out so fast that it can carry small boats far into Bass Strait.

Old hands talk matter-of-factly about the contours of the broad valley that lies under this sheet of water. Earlier this morning, one of my companions produced a map and showed me the old riverbeds where the shipping channels run. They've only been under water for 9000 years, a blink in the eye of geological time. He talked of diving around the gorge where the river used to flow through the Rip, and of riding the current down a drowned waterfall. This bay's history is below the surface, but it's not that far down.

When we head for home, I can see the spine of the landscape as I never can in town. The hills connect along the horizon to form the boundary of a large, shallow valley, with the bay in the centre like water in a bowl. It's easy to imagine that this was once dry land.

The distant hills slip out of sight as we come closer to shore. To our right, white buildings mark the water's edge, with the muted reds and greens of the suburbs spreading behind.

We nose into the river and under the West Gate Bridge. On the docks, tall cranes are lifting containers, red and blue and yellow in the sun. The banks are closer on each side, but we're not following the old river now. This is a canal, dug straight and deep by men with picks and shovels more than a century ago. When they'd finished here, they gouged out the river delta to form Victoria Dock, now called Victoria Harbour and lined with apartment towers.

Looking up the Yarra River across the rapids in the 1830s, painted from memory by W. F. E. Liardet

Slower now, we pass under bridges full of cars and trucks as we approach the city centre. At the bottom of Queen Street, the river widens to form a basin – all that's left of the place where sailing ships used to moor. I've seen paintings of this place as it used to be, with the river cascading down a set of rapids into a deep pool. That landscape is almost impossible to imagine now. The rapids have been blasted away, turning the river brackish far upstream. It's always struck me as strange that people went to such lengths to obliterate Melbourne's reason for being where it is.

When I get out in the centre of town, I'm plunged into the sights and sounds of a city where everything is on the move. Here, the past is buried deep under layer after layer of human constructions. But that sense of layering was what drew me to Melbourne in the first place almost 30 years ago. You can read the past in this city, if you know where to look.

ONE

KULIN COUNTRY

Near where I live is a hole in the fabric of the city – a deep bend in the Maribyrnong River that was the site of the Commonwealth Explosives Factory. The river flats are littered with brick buildings, many of them surrounded by mounds of earth in case something went bang. Ever since the factory closed, they've been debating what to do with the land. The buildings have asbestos roofs, and the soil is tainted with benzene and heavy metals; the local eels are so rich in polychlorinated biphenyls that you're warned not to eat them more than once a month.

But you can see that this was once a bountiful place. The river, salty and tidal now, would have been fresh before the sea level rose. The bend remains a haven for waterbirds, and there are edible plants along the edge. The grasslands in the valley would have supported plenty of game; even now, you occasionally see a snake or an echidna or a wallaby. Back when they built the factory in 1909, the builders found huge numbers of stone tools. Now we know how long this land has been inhabited, you can only speculate about what they were digging up.

The silcrete quarry above the Maribyrnong, and (below) a close-up showing the grooves in the stone

High on the other side of the river, just off the path that leads down to Steele Creek, is a rocky outcrop with a rounded top. In dry seasons, you can see the underside of the rock has been hollowed out to form a deep overhang. Stone was quarried here – hard, fine-grained silcrete, used for sharpening implements made of softer stone. From close up, you can see the grooves made by countless generations of people honing their tools on the rock.

This is the country of the Marin-balag, a family group of the Woiwurrung people, who were part of the Kulin nation. It was their uncontested territory for at least 1600 generations. The story of their dispossession is part of the city's history. When I stand on the edge of the valley and look downstream to the city towers, what I see is an invasion corridor.

The country around the bay belonged to three groups who intermarried and spoke a common language: the Wathawurrung in the south-west, the Woiwurrung in the north, and the Boonwurrung in the south-east and along the coast to the Werribee River. The Kulin were here during the last Ice Age, when the river they called Bar-ray-rung, 'river of mist', flowed out far beyond the southern horizon. They were here when the sea rose to form the bay, and they saw the water fall back to its present level about a thousand years ago.

People adapted to these changes of climate and country. They made cloaks of possum skin to protect them from the cold, wove nets to catch waterbirds, and built traps and channels in the rivers to steer fish into their baskets. They periodically burnt the vegetation to keep the country open and encourage grass to grow. Women harvested plants in the valleys; one of their staple crops was murnong, a flat-leafed plant with a yellow flower and a tuber that was a good source of starch. In the woodlands were manna gums where insects dropped a sweet secretion so thick that it sometimes frosted the ground white. People could feed, clothe and shelter themselves, making all their own tools, by working about 30 hours a week.

The Maribyrnong valley, with the defunct Commonwealth Explosives Factory in the foreground and the towers of central Melbourne rising behind

Kulin mostly moved around their country in family groups, but they met in larger numbers for ceremony and exchange. This bend in the Maribyrnong was probably one such meeting place. Another lay on the eastern branch of the river, where fresh water ran over a rocky bar. The Kulin called this place Narm. With its permanent water and plenty of food, it was a refuge, a place for ceremony, a place to be cared for.

It was also well hidden from the sea. Even the bay escaped notice for some years after 1788, when the British began sending convicts to Sydney, though news of the strangers' arrival doubtless travelled south. With it came new diseases, which far outpaced the spread of European settlement. A smallpox epidemic struck in 1790, and a second 40 years later. The Kulin spoke of how a giant serpent had come from the north breathing fumes so poisonous that people ran away in panic, not even pausing to honour their dead. Each time disease struck, the number of Kulin was halved; the death rate was even higher among women, so the losses were slow to make up. There were about 5000 people around the bay in the 1830s, but their original numbers may have been four times that.

About ten years after the first epidemic, sailing ships began to appear at the head of the bay. On 4 January 1802, Lieutenant John Murray saw the bay on his way to Bass Strait and sent a launch in. He returned in mid-February, and this time sailed into the bay in his ship, the *Lady Nelson*. He remarked on the beauty of the country, with its open woodlands and rolling hills. From the large number of fires, he judged that the bay was 'not thin of inhabitants', but he could not spot a river of any size.

The Boonwurrung, whose country this was, stayed out of sight for two days, then a group of men dressed in possum-skin cloaks met up with Murray's party. They accepted some gifts, but pointedly ignored the intruders' questions about where to find water. The situation became tense; the Boonwurrung produced spears, and Murray turned his guns on them. They fled, and had nothing more to

A watercolour by John Cotton of a Kulin camp beside the Yarra, c. 1845

do with the Europeans. Murray spent several weeks in the bay, fruitlessly seeking a channel to the north. Before he left, he claimed the country for Britain and raised the flag on shore, but he removed it again before nightfall in case the Boonwurrung took it down for him. His territorial claim was hollow, and he'd found no water.

Six weeks later, a much larger ship came through the heads and promptly ran aground. This was the *Investigator*, commanded by Matthew Flinders on his voyage around the continent he named Australia. The crew dragged the vessel free, but it could go nowhere in the shallow water. Unaware of Murray's visit, Flinders was puzzled that the local people seemed to be avoiding him. Though he could see their fires, every campsite he approached was empty. One day three Boonwurrung men met him on the shore, possibly by chance; they were friendly, but he noted with surprise that they did not flinch when he shot a bird. This was his only contact with the local people.

Seeking a view over the port, Flinders climbed a hill in the east (Murray, who had been there before him, had named it Arthur's Seat), then crossed to the western shore and climbed the tallest peak of the You Yangs. From the top, he could see a harbour big enough to shelter 'a larger fleet of ships than ever yet went to sea', but he returned to the *Investigator* parched and exhausted, having found nothing to drink along the way. He left

'The hills and valleys rise and fall with inexpressible elegance. We discovered no water nor any new wood of consequence, but it is impossible that a great want of water can be here from the number of native huts and fires we fell in with in our march.'
–JOHN MURRAY'S JOURNAL, 16 FEBRUARY 1801

a few days later without exploring the northern shore.

Next summer, in January 1803, a much smaller ship arrived: the *Cumberland*, only ten metres long, crowded with seventeen men. The acting chief surveyor of New South Wales, Charles Grimes, had been sent to take a closer look at the land around Port Phillip, as it had now been named. Grimes was a man of few words; we mainly know of the expedition's progress from the journals of James Flemming, a convict gardener sent out to assess the agricultural potential of the land.

It was early February by the time the little ship reached the northern shore and found the 'Great River', as Flemming called it. Next morning, a surveying party set out to row up the stream. When it divided into two, they took the western arm – the Maribyrnong – rather than the scrub-covered branch to the east. But the river was salty a long way up, and the country around it was dry. To the west was a treeless plain, where Flemming pronounced the soil 'very bad'. After crossing the river where it turned fresh, at 'a place the natives had made for catching fish' (later called Solomon's Ford), the party set off on foot to explore the valley. They found a few good pools of fresh water, but a thunderstorm turned them back.

Next day they rowed down to the junction and went up the scrubby eastern arm. A few miles upstream, they found the place where the water turned fresh. Here there was plenty of water and timber, and from a little hill beside the river they could see grasslands 'fit to mow'. Lacking other inspiration, Grimes called the stream the Freshwater River.

As the expedition proceeded, several groups of Kulin made fleeting contact with the surveyors; the exchanges were amicable, and no guns were fired. From Flemming's terse record, it's clear that the Kulin understood the use of metal. On the south-western shore, a group of Wathawurrung men expressed pleasure when Grimes offered a tomahawk as a gift, and two of them persuaded Flemming to part with his metal buttons. When the Europeans left, they discovered that someone had swum out to the boat and absconded with an iron hoe.

Although Flemming noted that the bar on the Freshwater River was 'the most eligible place for a settlement I have seen', his report was generally pessimistic about Port Phillip's prospects. Yet it was only a matter of months before yet another British expedition came through the heads, this time much larger and evidently intending to stay. Knowing nothing of Grimes's survey, the British government had sent Lieutenant-Governor David Collins out from England to establish a convict station in Port Phillip. He arrived in October 1803 with a party of 458 people, including 308 convicts, and made camp east of the entrance, at a place he called Sullivan Bay.

Short of water for his party, Collins sent James Tuckey out to search for a river. He could have chosen better; like Murray before him, Tuckey was quick to resort to force. When he encountered a group of men who seemed angry at his presence, he turned his guns on them, killing one man and sending the rest running into the bush. From then on, Tuckey stuck to his boat, afraid to venture ashore. He spotted the delta at the head of the port, but didn't go up it. On his return to Sullivan Bay, he persuaded Collins that the north was too dangerous to settle because it was 'full of natives' and had no permanent river.

At Sullivan Bay, the settlers had only the water that seeped into half a dozen wooden casks set in the sand. Once summer came, they experienced days of parching thirst.

'Started at six and came to the branch we passed before, at the entrance the land swampy; a few miles up found it excellent water, where we saw a little hill and landed. The time dinner was getting ready Messrs. Robbins, Grimes and self went on the hill, where we saw ... a large swamp between two rivers; fine grass, fit to mow; not a bush in it. The soil is black rich earth about six to ten inches deep ...'
– JAMES FLEMMING'S JOURNAL,
4 FEBRUARY 1803

During the worst heat wave, when bushfires roared through the surrounding hills and threatened their camp, the temperature reached 47°C.

Collins had already decided to abandon the place. Port Phillip, he reported, was 'wholly unfit' for settlement because it was 'entirely destitute of that great essential: fresh water … Every day's experience convinces me that it cannot, nor ever will be, resorted to by speculative men'. Late in January 1804, he loaded the entire party into two ships and set sail for Tasmania.

After that, the authorities refused to let anyone take up land in Port Phillip for more than 30 years. While settlers extended their hold over the land around Sydney and waged war against the people of Tasmania, few intruders came to bother the Kulin. Ships sometimes sheltered inside the bay's entrance or ran aground, and on at least one occasion sealers abducted women to work with them on the islands of Bass Strait. But the only official expedition to reach Port Phillip itself was in 1824, when Hamilton Hume and William Hovell came overland from Sydney. They went as far as Corio Bay, only to turn back after a tense encounter with the Wathawurrung. Hovell reported that the region had potential for grazing, and late in 1825 a short-lived outpost was formed on the shore of Westernport Bay to head off a French expedition under Dumont D'Urville. But again the reports were unfavourable and the government reiterated its position: there would be no legal settlement in Port Phillip.

Collins's failed attempt in 1803, however, had left two unexpected legacies. In the desperate days before the departure, three convicts got away. Two died, and the third, a man called William Buckley, was close to death when he was rescued by a group of Wathawurrung. They cared for this strange white giant – Buckley was about two metres tall – and he eventually adopted their language so completely that he almost forgot his native tongue. He was still there in 1835, when a new wave of intruders began to poke around Port Phillip Bay.

The other legacy of Collins's expedition was in the person of John Pascoe Fawkner, whose father was a convict at Sullivan Bay. Though only eleven years old at the time, Fawkner never forgot the days of thirst that summer. He was in his mid-forties before he thought of returning to Port Phillip, but when he did, he knew what to look for. Hearing news in Launceston that adventurers were about to defy the authorities and take up land across Bass Strait, Fawkner organised a competing expedition. When the party sailed in July 1835 under John Lancey's command, Fawkner farewelled them with the words: 'Look out for fresh water'. This was the search that led them to the place called Narm.

TWO

DISPOSSESSION

John Batman is a shadowy figure. He wrote little, died young, and never sat for a portrait. No reliable likeness of him survives.

Batman was a first-generation Australian, born in Sydney in 1801. In his youth, he became adept at the hybrid language of the frontier, where black and white communicated in a mixture of signs and words borrowed from each other's languages. He would later try to make this skill his passport to wealth.

As a young man, Batman became a grazier in Tasmania, where he helped the government with its scheme to put an end to rural violence by persuading Aboriginal people to leave their country peacefully. The policy was disastrous for the island's Aboriginal people, but Batman's role won him the friendship of the former attorney-general, Joseph Gellibrand, and other prominent settlers who were concerned at the violence that had attended British colonisation of the island.

In 1834, hearing that an illegal settlement had already been established at Portland on the mainland coast, Batman floated a scheme to take up land closer at hand, around Port Phillip Bay. He proposed making a treaty with the inhabitants to guarantee them payment for the use of their land. The move was patently self-interested, but Batman's friends hoped it would win support from the humanitarian lobby in London. They formed a syndicate, the Port Phillip Association, to back the venture, and the lawyer Joseph Gellibrand drafted an agreement exchanging land for a regular supply of Western goods.

Batman sailed to Port Phillip in May 1835, taking some Sydney Aboriginal men along to help him negotiate the deal. He set up camp at Indented Head on the south-west shore of the bay, where he exchanged gifts with the Wathawurrung and allegedly obtained their marks on a copy of the agreement. He then travelled north and met a group of Woiwurrung and Boonwurrung elders, who he claimed made their marks on a similar treaty covering the land at the head of the bay.

Historians have established that most of the negotiators involved in this second 'treaty' were senior clan members. It seems they had made a considered decision to deal with the stranger rather than embark on a potentially bloody course of resistance. They probably thought Batman merely wanted access to their country; it was unthinkable that he might seek exclusive ownership of what was self-evidently their land.

Batman's notes of this journey are sketchy, and it is hard to say where the second agreement was made. It may have been on the banks of Merri Creek, on Darebin Creek or even the Plenty River. For the same reason, there are questions over his later claim that he travelled to the pool in the Freshwater River and pronounced it 'the place for a village'. Some historians doubt that he went there at all.

When Batman returned to Launceston, he was feted as the largest landowner in the world, but things almost immediately began to sour. Rivals got wind of his scheme and began to organise their own sorties to the mainland. Batman himself fell ill (he was suffering from syphilis), so it was left to another member of the Port Phillip Association, the surveyor John Wedge, to map the country Batman had claimed.

Wedge had barely left for Port Phillip in August when the syndicate discovered that Richard Bourke, the governor of New South Wales, had declared the treaties void. His objection was not that a few blankets, trinkets and rations were miserly compensation for handing over 600,000 acres of country. Rather, Bourke enunciated the doctrine of *terra nullius* (literally 'nobody's land'): he argued that the Kulin could not dispose of the country because it was not theirs to sell. It was the property of the British Crown. The Colonial Office confirmed this decision two months later, in spite of lobbying by the syndicate's London friends. Any European settlement in Port Phillip was now clearly illegal.

Meanwhile, the syndicate's competitors had mustered. Wedge disembarked at Indented Head and travelled overland up the bay with some Wathawurrung men to guide him, but when they reached the bar on the river, John Lancey was already there with Fawkner's party, cutting down trees and building a wooden hut to use as a store. There was an argument. Wedge told Lancey he was trespassing and ordered him to leave, but Lancey refused, pointing out that Wedge's title was no more legal than his own. Before Wedge trudged off, he named the river 'Yarra Yarra', adopting the term his Wathawurrung guide had used for the flowing water at the rapids.

When Wedge broke the news that Fawkner's men had beaten him to the river, Batman, Gellibrand and others were all for defending their claim by force, or 'instigating the Natives' to drive Fawkner's party off. Wedge opposed any such course of action. The argument fractured the Port Phillip Association, and some of its members left.

Fawkner himself arrived on the river in October. Soon afterwards, several hundred Kulin converged on the place, expecting to meet Batman, but found his rival there instead.

They debated what to do. Fawkner had no right to be there in terms of local law: he hadn't been ceremonially introduced to the country or exchanged gifts with his hosts. The Wathawurrung and the Daungwurrung, who came from further north, were all for getting rid of the intruder, but the Boonwurrung and Woiwurrung resisted the idea.

Fawkner's main local ally was Derrimut, a senior member of the Yalukit-willam family of the Boonwurrung, whose mother's country included the land around Narm. Derrimut exchanged names with Fawkner and called him

John Batman's house on the hill as W. F. E. Liardet remembered it, with Benbow and Kitty's cottage in the garden by the river at lower right

his brother; the historian Richard Broome interprets this as a sign that Derrimut had decided to legitimise Fawkner's presence and establish a relationship of mutual obligation between them. Fawkner in turn gave Derrimut a knife, some Western clothes and the use of a gun.

By November 1835, John Batman was sufficiently recovered to return to Port Phillip, where he joined Fawkner by the Yarra. The two men agreed to co-exist: Fawkner would move his farm to the south bank of the river but keep the cottage he'd built on the other side. Batman too built a house near the river, on the little hill that Flemming and Grimes had climbed; he grazed his stock on the low-lying land around the wetlands to the west and established a depot to pay tribute as the treaty prescribed. A senior Yalukit-willam man whom the Europeans knew as Benbow moved in with his wife, who was known as Kitty, taking up a cottage at the bottom of Batman's garden.

Among those who assembled to greet John Batman was the escaped convict William Buckley, who had revealed his identity to the syndicate's men at Indented Head some months before. Buckley became the settlement's interpreter, and in early December he found himself acting as an intermediary for warnings of an impending attack. Once again there were differences between Kulin from up the country and the people of the river. Derrimut conveyed the warning, but he had the support of several senior men from the local clans, including Benbow and Billibellary, a signatory to Batman's treaty.

The settlers were convinced the threat was serious. Women and children had vanished, and warriors were concealing spears beneath their cloaks or dragging them along the earth between their toes. Fearing the Kulin intended to 'Kill and eat us all', Fawkner went out with some of his men, armed and on horseback, and fired his gun into a tree. The next day, he and his men again knocked off work 'and took our pieces to chase the Blacks'. Their show of force forestalled the attack.

For some time after that, Fawkner tried to deter Kulin from visiting the settlement. In February 1836 he noted with disgust that Batman had sent for 'a tribe of Aborigines to Show to Messrs Gellibrand & co', who were anxious to prove that their treatment of the Kulin had been humane. About a hundred people arrived, much to Fawkner's annoyance: 'Before this we had nearly got rid of them all'.

In fact, the European village became a magnet for the local people. Richard Broome has described it as a 'place of plenty', where Kulin could not only exchange possum skins, spears, baskets, tea-tree brooms and firewood for European goods, but were also offered gifts by right as payment for the use of their land. The most prized presents were guns for hunting; within a few years, about a third of the Kulin men around the settlement owned firearms.

The mutual curiosity of Kulin and Europeans helped bridge the cultural divide. The settlement attracted people from up the country, who escorted Europeans back to show them their land. In the late 1830s, it seems many such agreements were struck over a drink at the tavern Fawkner let out to the Melbourne Club. Guided by local people, Europeans and their sheep moved rapidly across the grasslands north and west of the town. Their main stock route ran up the east bank of the Maribyrnong, crossing the river where it turned fresh at Solomon's Ford.

But not all of the European graziers observed protocol in gaining the traditional owners' consent before moving their sheep into new country. One of the roughest was a man named Charles Franks, who moved into Mount Cottrell, west of the settlement. Franks refused to have anything to do with the local people; he took the land by force, and called his bullets 'blue pills for the natives'. In July 1836, barely a week after his arrival, he and one of his shepherds were found hacked to death, with their stock and possessions gone.

The incident convulsed the settlement. A town meeting resolved to 'deal with the Murderers' by enlisting 'as many Natives as would consent to go' on a retaliatory expedition. Next day, after a funeral for Franks and the shepherd, the expedition set off. Derrimut and a handful of local men rode out to Mount Cottrell, with Gellibrand and Wedge leading a much larger contingent of settlers. Fawkner supplied arms and ammunition, but did not take part. What happened next was not publicly reported, but it's believed at least

'Not a night but some one or another of the natives return to the encampment in a state of intoxication. I am informed by them and others that they obtain the liquor from a Mr Lee in the settlement. From their description it must be the club house.'
– WILLIAM THOMAS TO WILLIAM LONSDALE, 9 NOVEMBER 1839

ten Kulin were killed when the party fired on a group of 50 people.

Even before reports of this violence filtered north to Sydney, Governor Bourke had decided that the settlement in Port Phillip must be brought under control. In September 1836, William Lonsdale arrived to take charge as police magistrate, and one of his first tasks was to produce an official return of the land that had been illegally occupied. He found that Europeans had moved up the frontages of the Werribee and Moorabool rivers, and had occupied the Maribyrnong valley as far as Sunbury, where Fawkner's associate George Evans was ensconced at Emu Bottom. (The remains of his station are still standing.) In all, the district had 177 European inhabitants and 26,500 sheep.

This was the beginning of a land-grab that escalated far beyond Lonsdale's control. Four years later, the village had grown into a town of 10,000 people, and the district's sheep population had risen to 1.3 million. Squatters had taken over huge tracts of country, sweeping aside any suggestion that it was not their land. The authorities could do little to stop them. Port Phillip became the fastest moving of all Australian frontiers, and perhaps the bloodiest; Richard Broome has estimated that violence claimed the lives of more than a thousand Aboriginal people and about a hundred Europeans.

The Kulin's traditional economy was battered as their land was taken away. Sheep and cattle fouled water supplies and extinguished edible plants. As early as 1839, sympathetic Europeans reported that the loss of murnong was creating great distress around Mount Disappointment, 60 kilometres to the north. A few years later, a European observer quoted a Kulin man as saying, 'No yam at Port Phillip, too much by one white man bullock and sheep, all gone murnong'. The Kulin were left with few options but to take sheep for food, risking retribution, or to seek sustenance as best they could in town.

Though an Aboriginal protectorate came into operation in 1839, the protectors had no power to stop the land rush. With displaced people converging on Melbourne – 300 in 1838, 675 by 1844 – the campsites around the town became refugee camps. Living conditions were overcrowded, rations inadequate and diseases rampant. William Thomas, the assistant protector who tended to the refugees, despaired at the authorities' indifference.

Official policy was increasingly based on exclusion, backed by the use of force. Charles La Trobe, who was appointed superintendent of Port Phillip in 1839, believed his best chance of maintaining order was to keep Kulin and whites apart. In that year, the authorities broke up camps

'Sixteen stations I visited and at but one, a Mr Airey, did I find a philanthropic feeling and regard for [the Aborigines]. At two out of the 16 I found skulls of Aborigines placed over the doors of the huts as if to warn the lawful owners of the land at their peril to approach.'
– CHARLES SIEVWRIGHT, ASSISTANT PROTECTOR OF ABORIGINES, ON A VISIT TO MOUNT MITCHELL, APRIL 1839

'The Aborigines were necessarily greatly distressed for food, owing to the destruction of the "murnong" … now entirely cropped off by the sheep and cattle. … It was only under the pressure of hunger that they were ever disposed to meddle with the flocks.'
– E. S. PARKER, ASSISTANT PROTECTOR OF ABORIGINES, AT MOUNT DISAPPOINTMENT, 16 MARCH 1839

on the south bank and at Tromgin, later the site of the Botanic Gardens. Aboriginal people were forbidden to own guns, and their firearms were confiscated.

Once the farms and pastoral stations were fenced, Kulin lost the freedom to move around their country. East of the settlement, John Gardiner set armed men to guard his crops by the Yarra each night; at Bulleen, farmers around the Bolin Swamp insisted Woiwurrung be moved off for taking the potatoes left after harvest – though, as William Thomas noted, in England these leavings were a labourer's right.

Many of those who had experienced the easy-going atmosphere of the early settlement were no longer there to witness these efforts to turn it into an all-white space. Gellibrand disappeared on an expedition to the west in 1837. At the end of that year, William Buckley resigned from his position as interpreter. Disillusioned with the new administration and fearing for his adopted people, he left Port Phillip, never to return. By that stage John Batman too was on the outer. When he died in May 1839 at barely 38 years of age, he was in debt, estranged from his wife, crippled and disfigured by disease, and still fruitlessly petitioning the government to grant him the hill where he had built his home.

Derrimut outlived most of the Europeans who had intruded on his country, but his existence became increasingly marginal. At first he worked with Fawkner, hunting with him, helping with his boat, and learning the trade language of the frontier. In August 1836, soon after the death of Charles Franks, Fawkner decided to flee the looming violence and return to Tasmania, and Derrimut went with him. In Hobart, Derrimut was introduced to Governor Arthur and had his portrait painted; he also appears to have indulged in some heavy drinking. He returned to Port Phillip with Fawkner four months later.

By the late 1830s, Derrimut was living in the town camp, periodically alarming the puritanical William Thomas by turning up drunk. Sometimes he went off to the eastern parts of his country, where the dense forests had deterred European settlement. In 1839, he was among a group of senior Boonwurrung men who took the botanist Daniel Bunce through the Dandenong Ranges to Westernport Bay, showing him how rich their country was and just how well they lived there. A few years later, he was conveying messages to the Daungwurrung on behalf of the chief protector, and there are several accounts of him conducting ceremonies around the settlement.

But the town became a hostile place in the 1840s, with La Trobe repeatedly ordering the protectors to break up the camps. Derrimut met the magistrate William Hull in Collins Street one day and pointed to the Bank of Victoria, saying, 'You see, Mr Hull, Bank of Victoria, all this mine, all along here Derrimut's once.' When Hull asked whether he had children, Derrimut replied angrily, 'Why me have lubra? Why me have picanninny? You have all this place, no good have children, no good have lubra, me tumble down and die very soon now.'

The protectorate collapsed in 1850 under the weight of white hostility, and in July 1851 the Port Phillip District officially became the colony of Victoria. The first gold discoveries were made public almost immediately, and a rush was soon under way. By 1854, Melbourne had 76,600 settlers.

In 1853, in the midst of the rush, La Trobe appointed William Thomas as the colony's sole Guardian of Aborigines. The two men informally agreed to set aside two areas of land for the Kulin: a patch on the eastern shore at Mordialloc for the Boonwurrung, and a larger area for the Woiwurrung at Warrandyte on the Yarra. Derrimut still visited the city at times, but he adopted Mordialloc as his base. The reserve was in his people's country, and the fishing there was good. William Thomas helped out with necessities from the government stores.

But during the late 1850s the Mordialloc reserve came under pressure from Chinese and European fishers, who took over the beach to salt snapper for the goldfields. The land had never been officially gazetted as an Aboriginal reserve, and by then La Trobe was no longer around to confirm his private agreement with Thomas. In 1861 the authorities incorporated the land into the Mordialloc common, ignoring Thomas's protests.

The Boonwurrung now had nowhere to turn, as all their land had been taken away. In 1863 a reserve was gazetted in the hills at Coranderrk, far outside their country, and the next week the Mordialloc land was put up for sale. William Thomas and John Fawkner formed a deputation to oppose the move, but their representations were ignored.

Derrimut stayed on at Mordialloc with a small group of Boonwurrung, but his life became increasingly dislocated. Though he was in his early fifties and in poor health, he often went to the city, where he was repeatedly imprisoned for drunkenness. By December 1863 he was nearly blind and his left arm was paralysed. After a period in and out of hospital, he was placed with other paupers in the Melbourne Benevolent Asylum. Fawkner visited him there; on one of these visits, Derrimut took his hand and said, 'Oh, my brother Johnny, long long time ago'.

William Thomas too continued to visit. On 16 April 1864, Derrimut's kin came up from Mordialloc to see him, but they had been drinking, and the teetotaller Thomas turned them away. Derrimut died nine days later, on 25 April. He was buried in Melbourne General Cemetery, and his role in saving the early settlers was memorialised on a headstone arranged by Fawkner, the man he had called his brother half a lifetime before.

The Pilchard Fishery at Williamstown, engraving by Samuel Calvert, 1865

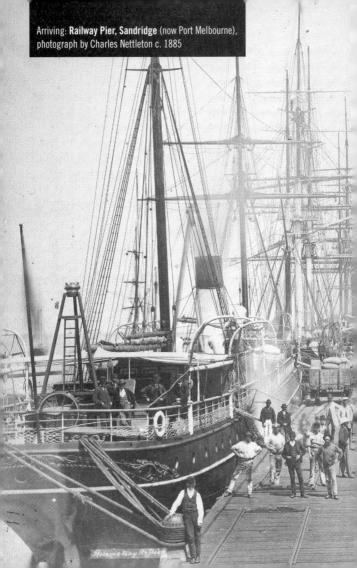

Arriving: **Railway Pier, Sandridge** (now Port Melbourne), photograph by Charles Nettleton c. 1885

THREE

REMAKING
THE LANDSCAPE

If Melbourne had a patron saint, it would have to be John Pascoe Fawkner, though in many ways he's an unlikely candidate. Mercurial, opinionated and tiny – just five feet two inches tall, in an age when people's social standing tended to match their physical size – Fawkner lived to become the settlement's elder statesman. He promoted urban interests against the powerful squatting lobby, and those of small farmers against the pastoral land monopoly. To his allies, he was the 'tribune of the people', but his well-padded enemies portrayed him as a demented leprechaun. There are many portraits of his thin, large-featured face with its hooded, knowing eyes.

In Melbourne, Fawkner made a fortune, lost it and made another. He handwrote the town's first newspaper and established its first library in his hotel. His books and newspapers caught the eye of Joseph Gellibrand, who had written Batman's 'treaty', and the two political opponents soon began sitting up late together, reading and discussing books.

John Fawkner as he liked to see himself; the image is from the visiting card he used in the 1860s

Like Batman, Fawkner was a convict's son made good. In Tasmania he had been a farmer, baker, publican, builder, nurseryman, coach-owner and newspaper proprietor. He had also been branded a criminal. In a moment of youthful idealism, he'd tried to help a group of convict workers escape, for which crime he was sentenced to 500 lashes and sent to New South Wales, where he spent two years cutting timber and burning lime. The experience destroyed any respect he might have had for the colonial authorities. While he built up his business in Launceston, he wrote a constitution for an imaginary place where citizens would be free of the 'so called English law'.

When Fawkner's party reached the Yarra, their first move was to plant food crops. John Lancey had chosen his base with care. He described it as a 'delightful spot', with fresh water, good soil and an abundance of grass. Fruit trees, vegetables and wheat were already in the ground before Fawkner arrived.

The diary Fawkner kept during his first year on the Yarra shows something of the man at work. On 16 October 1835, Fawkner and his wife Eliza arrived with their helpers in his ship the *Enterprize*, and the next day all the men began cutting timber to build a house and store. This activity consumed almost all their daylight hours until 7 November, when the new store was completed and Fawkner started unloading his goods.

There was no small quantity of cargo,

'Your Lordship has been fortunate in the lot I chose for you. A more delightful spot, I think, cannot be. Beautiful grass, a pleasant prospect, a fine fresh-water river ... A salt lagoon and piece of marsh will make a beautiful meadow and bounded on the south by the river. This hill is composed of a rich, black soil, thinly wooded with honeysuckle and she-oak. Good grass ... and geraniums in abundance.'
– JOHN LANCEY TO JOHN FAWKNER, AUGUST 1835

as we know from the notes he kept when the ship was loaded at Launceston. As well as bricks, shingles, palings, planks and other building materials, he'd brought butter, tea, a ton of flour, three casks of pork and two of beef, a cask of port, 25 gallons of gin, raisins, calico, six trunks and chests of clothes, and 'sundry Boxes of Books', as well as 20 bags of oats and a ton of hay to feed two horses, two cows and their calves.

Having put the stores under shelter, Fawkner and Eliza moved into the house, and for the next week he busied himself building cupboards and helping John Batman and his colleagues unload

W. F. E. Liardet's painting of John Fawkner's first house by the Yarra, with his Yalukit-willam allies camped in the garden and his wheatfield on the south bank of the river

their ships. He punctuated the daily grind with trips to fish in the bay or hunt in the wetlands. On 17 November he dined on a 'sea pie' made from 24 of the wading birds he called sand snipe.

The next day, having agreed to move his crops to the south bank, Fawkner selected a new farm site at the edge of a marsh, and agriculture began in earnest. His men started by digging out the trees and burning them. Over the next two days they ploughed the land and started planting potatoes, green beans, peas and radishes.

Fawkner now found a source of quick cash in wattle bark,

which was used in tanning animal skins. Light, valuable and easy to transport, the bark made an ideal export. In late November, he and his workers began to strip a stand of wattles four miles from the river. For weeks, they alternated between the bark ground and the farm, where Fawkner maintained a furious pace. His diary entry for 30 November reads:

> *Finished putting in potatoes and planted Cherry & Damson Stones & Apple Pips. Sowed Pea's, French Beans, Carrots, 2 Soils Turnip, Radish, Cauliflower and Savoy Cabbage Seeds and Curly Parsley – Planted Pumpkins, Melons, Vegetable Marrow and Cucumber Seeds. Mr Batman 5 Gall[on]s of Red Wine.*

He watered his plants from the river, and cleared and fenced another garden and a horse paddock. While he was about it, he had his men remove some trees in front of his house to 'open the View', much to the annoyance of his neighbour, John Batman's brother Henry, who refused to speak to him for several weeks.

When winter came, Fawkner planted a field of wheat. In his enthusiasm for farming, he often got ahead of himself; his cows and horses strayed, and his pigs uprooted his vegetable garden. He had hoped to breed rabbits, but fortunately they were shot by one of Henry Batman's men.

Fawkner's actions encapsulated a paradox of colonisation. He was a dedicated husbandman, and worked himself and his men hard. Throughout this period of tumultuous activity, he kept a daily record of the weather and noted the success or failure of every crop he planted. He also understood the local seasons. His manic efforts in November were driven by the knowledge that summer was fast approaching, and he was late in planting because of the delay in settling on the site for his farm.

Yet this ethic of husbandry only extended to the plants and animals he had brought with him. His approach to the local flora and fauna was one of opportunistic exploitation. He and his men barked wattles, cut down gums, ploughed in native grasses and shot birds and kangaroos, with never a thought that these too might repay husbandry.

In 1839, Fawkner bought a large area of land along the Moonee Creek. He used his newspaper, the *Port Phillip Patriot*, to advertise for tenant farmers in this 'ROMANTIC, RUSTIC and SYLVAN' valley around the 'beautiful village of Pascoe'. Here too Fawkner did his bit to 'improve' the scenery. He leased part of his estate to his father on condition that the elder Fawkner 'fell cut down grub up and otherwise destroy and remove all the native indigenous trees wood scrub and underwood whatsoever growing or to grow upon the said land or any part thereof'.

Fawkner was not the only new arrival who brought a crusading zeal to the task of making Port Phillip look like home. The Scots imported their thistles, the English their briars and sparrows and rabbits. These efforts became more systematic after 1861, when the editor of the *Argus* newspaper, Edward Wilson, established an Acclimatisation Society to promote the introduction of new species. He was especially keen to bring in European songbirds to alleviate the 'savage silence' of the Australian bush. The society promoted the introduction of trout, carp, llamas, camels and cashmere goats, among others. Specimens were put on display in Melbourne's Zoological Gardens, which the society ran on a site in Royal Park donated by the government in 1862.

In the botanical arena, one of the most energetic promoters of acclimatisation was Ferdinand von Mueller, who became Government Botanist in 1853, a position he later combined with directing the Botanic Gardens. Von Mueller used the gardens to educate the public about new plants. His gardens were densely planted in geometrical avenues to display the botanical treasures of the world, meticulously labelled, and he promoted the cause by distributing thousands of free specimens. But the Melbourne public sought recreation as well as education in the gardens, and in 1873 von Mueller was dislodged in favour of William Guilfoyle, who replaced the dense plantings with wide lawns, a fern gully and winding paths.

Ferdinand von Mueller with a chest full of medals, photographed in 1900

In spite of being deposed as director of the gardens, von Mueller stayed on in Melbourne, where he continued to pursue the international exchange of plants. He believed this should be a two-way trade: he not only encouraged the importation of useful species, but also promoted the virtues of Australian plants – especially gum trees, which he exported to California, India and elsewhere, confident they would help in 'obliterating the rainless areas of the globe'. His reputation as an expert on Australian plants won him numerous honours, including a hereditary baronetcy bestowed in 1871 by the King of Württemberg.

Von Mueller was critical of excessive land-clearing, but his chiding had little effect on Victoria's farmers and graziers. Government policies required smallholders to clear trees as proof that they had 'improved' their blocks. And the squatters, who ran their sheep across huge pastoral stations leased cheaply from the Crown, had no incentive to conserve the country.

Even among the first generation of settlers, there were many who realised that the countryside was being degraded. Barely fifteen years after taking up his property in the Western District, squatter John Robertson recorded that the native grasses were dying out, leaving the soil exposed. But the squatters and the farmers countenanced this destruction – the cutting down of forests, the erosion of watercourses, the extinction of

'The long deep-rooted grasses that held our strong clay hill together have died out; the ground is now exposed to the sun, and it has cracked in all directions, and the clay hills are slipping ... also the sides of precipitous creeks – long slips, taking trees and all with them.'
– JOHN ROBERTSON IN *Letters from Victorian Pioneers*, 1854

native plants' – in the pursuit of short-term gain, justifying it as the price of progress. And by the time their children had come into their own, the degradation of the country was a fait accompli. Johnny Fawkner, toiling in his few acres by the Yarra, seems a model of integrity by comparison.

FOUR

IN THE GRID

When Fawkner returned to the Yarra at the end of 1836, the first thing he saw beside the wharf was a whipping post. While he was away in Hobart, William Lonsdale had arrived as police magistrate, and the settlement now included 33 soldiers, a party of convict labourers, three police and a scourger. For Fawkner, who had felt the lash as a young man, there could be no more potent symbol of the authorities' determination to tame the unruly village.

When Lonsdale arrived, settlers had been in Port Phillip for more than a year without the guiding hand of the state. A town meeting the previous June had appointed James Simpson to adjudicate disputes and petitioned Governor Bourke to appoint a police magistrate. But the problems were not confined to resolving quarrels among the settlers, or even to policing their relations with the Kulin. The settlers had no legal right to the land they were occupying. The village did not even have an official name. It was variously called Dutigalla, after the territory covered by Batman's second treaty, Bearbrass, Bareheap or Bareburp, from the word for Yalukit-willam land, or simply the Settlement.

The land question required the personal attention of Governor Bourke, who duly visited in March 1837. Bourke saw it as his mission to 'extend the power of order and social union to the most distant parts of the wilderness', including this raggle-taggle village. Within a week, he swept it aside with a stroke of his pen. Over the top of its scattered houses and winding tracks, he had the surveyor Robert Hoddle draw up a grid of straight, wide streets to form the framework of a new town. The only buildings spared were Batman's house and Fawkner's hotel. Everyone else was given a month to get out. It was Bourke who named the settlement Melbourne, after the British prime minister of the time.

Bourke's startling intervention established the outlines for a town that would be modern in more that one sense. Like a military camp, it was designed for surveillance and ease of movement, with no narrow alleys where restive elements could congregate out of the authorities' sight. The main streets were laid out as boulevards 99 feet wide, and the land subdivided into long blocks, serviced by access lanes at the back. There would be no deviations from the relentless geometry of the grid to accommodate trees, hills or creeks. These straight lines on paper represented an imagined landscape; historian Kathryn Ferguson describes it as a vision of order that simply was not there.

Not surprisingly, this vision was difficult to translate into reality. For more than a decade after 1837, the verdant landscape of central Melbourne was reduced to a building site. Road-making gangs spent much of their time felling ancient gum trees. Stumps littered the streets, and when they were uprooted they left cavernous holes, which turned into lakes in wet weather. To make matters worse, the streets were perfectly aligned to catch the prevailing winds. The cold south-westerlies brought rain from the sea in winter, and in summer hot north-westerlies from the interior raised dust clouds so thick they blotted out the sun.

Drainage was non-existent. Elizabeth Street ran along a creek that joined the river above the rapids, and its flow was boosted by run-off from the main streets spearing down the hills on each side. It was christened the River Townend, and Queen Street the River Enscoe, after two local merchants. A third gave his name to Lake Cashmore, a waterhole on the corner of Collins and Elizabeth Streets where urchins lay in wait at night, hoping to waylay unwary policemen and push them in.

When the river rose, Flinders Street became a swamp, especially around the wharves. The *Port Phillip Patriot* complained that wading through the city was a Herculean task. The mud was so deep that even bullocks got stuck. A storm in the early 1850s produced such a torrent that a horse was swept off its feet and drowned outside the General Post Office; ten years later, people still occasionally drowned in the streets.

The land market too defied Bourke's orderly vision. Once the grid was laid out, long blocks on the main streets were auctioned in June 1837. (Surveyor Hoddle, who ran the auction, took the chance to buy some land, much to John Fawkner's disgust.) But once the authorities had sold the land, they surrendered control to private speculators with subdivision on their minds. As immigrants poured into Melbourne, the backs of these long city blocks were lopped off and sold separately. The 'little' streets became business precincts in their own right, each

'Wanted immediately: one thousand pairs of stilts for the purpose of enabling the inhabitants of Melbourne to carry on their usual avocations – the mud in most of the principal thoroughfares being now waist deep.'
– 1840 SPOOF ADVERTISEMENT, QUOTED IN GARRYOWEN, *The Chronicles of Early Melbourne*

The Oaks

S A L T   L A K E
at times quite dry

F L A T

Tea Tree & River

Tea Tree Scrub

Map

SHEWING THE SITE OF

MELBOURNE

and the position of the Dutch Building previous to the

foundation of the Township by Sir Richard Bourke,

in 1837.

M
20 Sydney

Scale 8 Inches to a Mile.

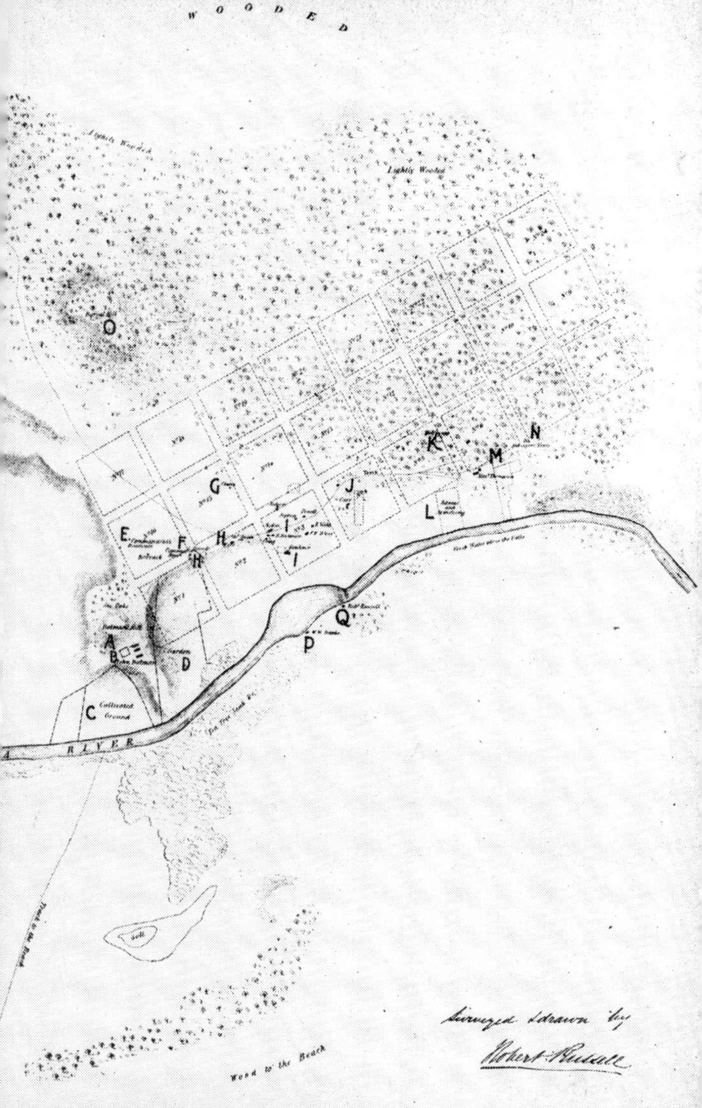

WOODED

Lightly Wooded

Lightly Wooded

O

K

N

M

G

J

L

E

F

H

T

I

Q

A

B

D

P

C Cultivated Ground

RIVER

Wood to the Beach

Surveyed & drawn by

Robert Russell

with its warren of even narrower alleys – exactly what the grid had been intended to avoid.

The surveyors faced a constant battle to regulate the use of land, as the influx of settlers soon spilt outside the grid. Beyond the surveyed zone in the centre was a labyrinth of dirt tracks lined with tents and temporary huts. Building materials were in such short supply that even the wealthiest colonists lived in houses made of prefabricated panels shipped in from overseas. When Georgiana McCrae arrived with her four children in 1841, she lived in a wooden cottage in Little Lonsdale Street consisting of one 'tolerably large' room with four 'closets (called bedrooms)' opening off it. Its walls and ceilings, made of thin panels imported from Singapore, offered little protection from the winter cold. Even La Trobe's cottage, built in 1839 and later moved to a site near the Botanic Gardens, was a superior version of what today would be called a kit home.

In *Bearbrass*, her book on the early settlement, Robyn Annear quotes an anonymous critic who summarised the surveyors' philosophy: 'the site must be made to suit the plan – not the plan to suit the site'. But in time the site *was* made to suit the plan. The mountainous trees were removed, streets levelled and houses built. Returning in April 1840 after less than two months up the country, squatter Niel Black found the town transformed as if 'a magic wand had been waved over it – where a forest stood when I left, there I found houses and streets on my return'. William Knight's romantic painting of Collins Street a few months later portrays it as a wide, treeless thoroughfare lined with houses and market gardens – and ending at Lake Cashmore, where it crossed Elizabeth Street.

The authorities found a temporary solution to the drainage problem in 1843, when they began building up the centres of the main streets so that water would run off to

COLLINS STREET.

Town of MELBOURNE, PORT PHILIP,

NEW SOUTH WALES.

Looking east up Collins Street in August 1840, as portrayed by William Knight

the sides. Even so, Elizabeth Street remained impassable after rain. It was not until the late 1870s that the government found a final solution in the master plan drawn up by British engineer Sir John Coode. In keeping with the terraforming philosophies of the time, Coode recommended reshaping the Yarra and its delta to human ends. His plan took more than a decade to implement. The rock that formed the Yarra rapids was blasted away, turning the river brackish far upstream. Its bed was dredged deeper and the banks built up, giving it the appearance of a canal. The run-off from Elizabeth Street could now be channelled into the river through an underground drain.

The delta was earmarked for even more radical treatment. The Melbourne Harbour Trust had already 'reclaimed' the lake known as Batman's Swamp by diverting the water that fed it from Moonee Ponds Creek. Once full of clear water, the swamp had become polluted beyond redemption, and it was filled during the late 1870s. But this was as nothing beside Coode's scheme, which involved digging a broad canal to bypass the shallow bend known as Humbug Reach, where the Yarra met the Maribyrnong, and constructing an artificial dock on the plain west of Flagstaff Hill. The new harbour opened as Victoria Dock in 1892. In the next phase, Appleton Dock was dug and the spoil used to fill the old riverbed, erasing it from the map.

Within the grid, the urban landscape had begun to differentiate into specialised

'Stretching away from the base of the Flag-staff Hill lay a beautiful blue lake … intensely blue, nearly oval and full of the clearest saltwater, but this, by no means deep. Fringed gaily all round by … "pigface" in full bloom, it seemed in the broad sunshine as though ringed about with a belt of magenta fire.'
— G. G. McCrae remembers Batman's Swamp in the settlement's early years

precincts. The seat of government and administration was on Eastern Hill, where an imposing Parliament House was swiftly built in time for the first sitting of parliament in 1856. Below it, medical practices and high-class shops gravitated towards the top end of Collins Street. On the opposite side of town, the slopes of Batman's Hill were home to banks, finance houses and a stock exchange. And where Swanston Street gently rose to the north, the public library marked the route to the university, which opened in 1855 on a capacious site outside the grid. Below these eminences of government, wealth and culture was a bustling valley of commerce, its shops full to bursting with commodities from around the world.

Churches too clustered in the city centre, encouraged by generous grants of land. At first the various Christian denominations shared a communal Pioneer Church in William Street, but in 1838 Lonsdale decided the Church of England should have exclusive rights to the building. The Anglicans later moved the wooden building aside to build the brownstone St James Cathedral, which opened in 1842. The Presbyterians meanwhile had been granted almost a hectare on the corner of Collins and Russell Streets, where the Scots' Church opened in 1841. In the same year, Melbourne's Catholics, who were worshipping in a building made of secondhand floorboards, began laying the foundations of St Francis' Church in Lonsdale Street. This was the city's cathedral until the late 1860s, when St Patrick's opened on Eastern Hill.

In its first two decades of existence, Melbourne did not experience continuous growth. There was a severe financial crisis

in the early 1840s after the initial land boom burst; ten years later the town was plunged into chaos when its men deserted for the goldfields, and there was another crisis in the late 1850s when the town was swamped by unemployed ex-miners, daily marching in the streets and chanting 'Give us bread'. But after each of these crises the city tapped new sources of wealth and came roaring back to life. Between 1846 and 1861, the settler population increased tenfold to reach 123,000. By the time John Fawkner died in 1869, the rude village among the gums had morphed into a landscape

John Fawkner's funeral procession in Spring Street, near the Bourke Street corner, October 1869

of wide streets, its skyline dominated by buildings of brick and stone.

The city centre grew steadily in the 1870s, then suddenly took off. Land values trebled between 1885 and 1888. Plain buildings were replaced by opulent multi-storey structures, and the introduction of powered elevators made it possible to construct 'skyscrapers' far higher than anything dependent on stairs. The city's tallest building, owned by the Australian Property and Investment Company, was twelve storeys tall and towered almost 50 metres above the corner of Elizabeth Street and Flinders Lane.

Even the churches felt the breath of speculation. In 1888, at the peak of the boom, the Catholic archbishop refused an offer of £140,000 for St Francis' Church. In the same year, the Anglicans were offered £300,000 for the incomplete St Paul's Cathedral on the corner of Swanston and Flinders Streets; bitterly divided, they only rejected the proposal by one vote.

The development of the railways reinforced the centrality of the grid. The first railway opened in September 1854 – a private line from the port to a collection of weatherboard buildings on Flinders Street. Within a few years, radial lines linked the centre to several of its suburbs: the St Kilda line began

Commuters toil up the wooden walkways of the old Flinders Street Station in 1890

operating in 1857, Windsor two years later, Brighton and Essendon in 1860 and Hawthorn in 1861. Further city stations opened at Princes Bridge and Batman's Hill in 1859, but they were not linked with Flinders Street until 1879, after the Victorian government had taken over the city's struggling private lines. Flinders Street Station itself remained a patchwork of unroofed platforms and makeshift buildings until the early twentieth century, when the railway authorities finally completed the massive domed structure that has become Melbourne's most distinctive landmark.

In the suburbs, passengers initially walked to the stations or were ferried by horse-drawn trams, but during the 1880s these began to give way to trams propelled by moving cables below street level. In 1885, a private company was given a 30-year monopoly over tram construction in the city; during the next five years, it built 75 kilometres of double track extending to Northcote, Toorak and Brighton. Though patronage increased rapidly, the cable trams were impractical over long distances. In 1920, five years after the company's monopoly expired, the lines were taken over by the government through the Melbourne and Metropolitan Tramways Board, which set about converting them to electricity.

The first electric tram, oddly enough, ran between the eastern suburbs of Box Hill and Doncaster; it opened in 1889 but folded seven years later, and today the only trace of its existence is the name of Tram Road, the north-south route along which it ran. The main electric network connecting the city centre with the suburbs began in 1906 with a private line to Essendon, and the last cable tram was converted to electricity in 1940. Over the course of the twentieth century, Melbourne's tram network expanded to become the largest in the world, with 245 kilometres of track.

It was not only the suburbs that were tied to the city centre. From 1859, country trains began linking the rural areas to the station at Batman's Hill (later Spencer Street, and still later Southern Cross). Regional railways to Geelong and Sunbury were built the same year, quickly followed by lines to Bendigo (1862), Echuca (1864),

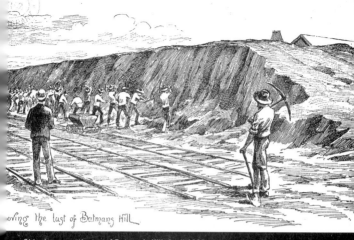

oving the last of Batmans Hill

Chipping away the top of **Batman's Hill**, April 1892

Seymour (1872) and Wodonga (1873). In the 1890s, the Spencer Street station was extended and Batman's Hill was beheaded, erasing yet another trace of the original landscape.

The city's hinterland even stretched beyond Victoria. Strategically placed lines tapped into the steamboat trade along the inland rivers to channel the rich pastoral business of the Riverina and western New South Wales towards the southern port. The railway to Echuca was connected to a private line running to Deniliquin in New South Wales. No matter what was produced in the countryside – wool, gold, grain, fruit or meat – much of it made its way to Melbourne.

As rural produce came in, manufactured goods went out. The metal trades thrived with the growth of demand for rails, boilers, rolling stock and agricultural machinery; brick-making, food processing, clothing manufacture, furniture-making, printing and boot-making all expanded to serve a rapidly increasing population. By 1891, about 30 per cent of Melbourne's workers were employed in manufacturing. The letterhead of one of the largest manufacturers, Lennon's agricultural implement works in Spotswood, featured the company's name set over a plume of black smoke.

But this proud polluter's location signalled a shifting balance. As manufacturing increased in scale, industries sought larger premises in Footscray, Spotswood and Brunswick. The centrifugal tendency accelerated in the twentieth century as motor vehicles came into wider use. Factories moved to Dandenong, Moorabbin, Broadmeadows and Geelong in the 1950s and 1960s, and to Laverton, Craigieburn, Bayswater and Pakenham after that. The population went with them – indeed, in the latter stages of the shift it was industry that followed the people rather than the other way around. Patterns of movement within the city broke away from the radial network of trams and railway lines. The central grid, once the gateway through which all traffic had to pass, now straddled a system that was falling into disuse.

The low point came in 1980, just after I moved to Melbourne, when the government received a report on transport policy from Murray Lonie, formerly of General Motors and BHP. Lonie recommended swingeing cuts to the fixed-rail network. Seven tram lines and six suburban rail lines were slated for closure, along with all the regional railways except the service to Geelong. To make sure the closures were permanent, the lines were to be torn up and sold for scrap.

The report's timing was unfortunate; just weeks before it was released, OPEC announced a sharp increase in the international price of oil. Combined with public protests, this forestalled many of the closures, including all but two of the suburban railway lines. But most of Lonie's other recommendations were eventually carried out: freeways were extended, freight deregulated to shift goods from rail to road, and an outer ring road built so that vehicles could travel from one side of Melbourne to the other and barely glimpse the inner city on the horizon.

Shifts in public employment accentuated the centre's decline. In the 1980s and 1990s, government departments came under pressure to cut staff numbers, and several institutions that had held the city together moved out of the grid. While government pondered how to rein in the spreading car-dependent suburbs, it was also dismantling one of the engines that had driven the inner city's growth. The centre of Melbourne was becoming less than central to the sprawling conurbation around it.

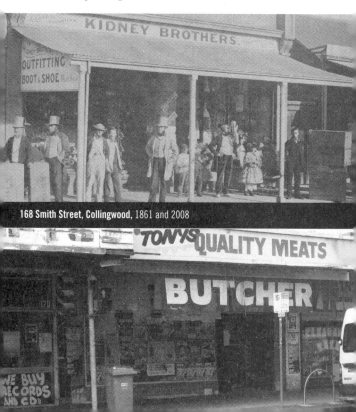

168 Smith Street, Collingwood, 1861 and 2008

FIVE

A COLLECTION
OF VILLAGES

In Moreland Road on the border of Brunswick and Coburg, not far from where I used to live, there's a hill with a view over the Moonee Creek. At the top of the hill is a wooden church, next to a row of shops; opposite is a weatherboard cottage – not a suburban villa, but a plain nineteenth-century farmhouse. For years it was in a state of disrepair – in fact, it seemed beyond repair.

I must have driven past that church and that cottage a hundred times without noticing them, except as a glitch among the newer houses along that stretch of road. It's different when you walk there, though. The first time I tackled that hill on foot, it was a hot day and a long haul, made longer by a four-year-old who was fascinated by every fence and a toddler who'd decided that pushers were passé. When we paused at the top, I suddenly realised where we were. The little wooden church (now at the back of a larger church) was once part of a village looking out over the market gardens along the creek. I could imagine the congregation standing around after the service: the women trading recipes and family news, the men

Looking west along Moreland Road from Glencairn Avenue in 1904

talking about the weather and the price of cabbages.

Melbourne's suburbs are full of places like this – old hamlets sticking up like islands in a sea of brick veneer. Large parts of the city are less like the suburbs of a centralised metropolis than a collection of villages that have gradually joined together. And each of these villages has its own archaeology, its own network of family and social relations, its own organisation of space, place and time. Together they make an impossibly complex urban landscape. You could spend a lifetime trying to pin it down, but it would beat you in the end.

I keep trying, though. I've spent hours poring over old Sands & McDougall's street directories, which not only tell you which houses were in a particular street in a particular year, but also list the householders' names and occupations. I've become better at dating houses from their architecture, and have disrupted numerous family outings by playing 'spot the chimney' at inappropriate times.

I first became interested in Melbourne's landscape when I was living near the hamlet on the hill, on the southern edge of Coburg (or Moreland, as the locals preferred to call it). Our house was a Californian bungalow built in 1926 on the low side of the street. The houses on the other side had been built a few years earlier. You could tell from Sands & McDougall, but you could also see the difference in the shingles on their gables: ours were scalloped, theirs were square.

Apart from these minor differences, the subdivision presented a remarkably uniform landscape of detached weatherboard houses with terracotta roofs. When the land was subdivided after World War I, most of the houses were financed by the State Bank, which was extremely prescriptive about design. If you wanted a bank loan for a new home, you had to use one of their plans, and in the 1920s that meant you had to build a Californian bungalow.

But there were still traces of what was there before the subdivision, when the area was farmland. There had once been a creek at the bottom of the valley; occasionally you'd meet an old-timer who could remember scrambling around its banks before it was put into a barrel drain. Next to it was a farmhouse, barely visible through the ivy; it didn't appear in the street directories until the 1880s, but it looked older than that.

Further up the hill was Glencairn, the house that had given its name to the subdivision and also to a local street. It had begun as a plain bluestone structure built in 1859 for Robert Mailer, a Melbourne merchant. The property stayed in the family for almost a hundred years, and its address had changed repeatedly as the suburb grew up around it. The earliest listing I found gave the address as Sydney Road, which was about a kilometre away. The house had been extended in the 1880s and again in 1911 to include four grand rooms at the front. It still occupied a large block of land, but was hemmed in by smaller houses. Its immediate neighbours, incongruously, were postwar cream brick veneers, built after the last strip of land was sold off. Even so, the dimensions of the house and garden made it easy to imagine that it had once stood at the end of a country lane.

Glencairn wasn't the oldest place in the south of Coburg, though; that honour went to a house tucked away in a side street on the hill above Moonee Creek. Originally called La Rose, it's probably the oldest dwelling in Victoria still on its original site. It was built about 1842 for Farquhar McCrae, a doctor, land speculator and gentleman about town. At the first local sale of land in 1839, McCrae bought a 600-acre holding, which he named Moreland after his grandfather's plantation in Jamaica. He later added the La Rose land, intending to build his homestead there.

McCrae's purchases were part of a speculative mania that overtook Melbourne in the late 1830s, spreading out from the central grid as more land was surveyed for sale. Blocks bought at Crown auctions changed hands at higher prices within months, weeks or even days. The cautious Scotsman Niel Black, who arrived in the midst of the bubble, labelled Port Phillip a 'land of credit' and condemned the shady practices he found. At land auctions a speculator would line up his associates to make inflated bids on his behalf, so that he was effectively selling the land to himself; these phantom sales might account for nine out of ten auction results. The exercise would turn a profit if just one or two new arrivals were

'This country is the land of credit … Everything has attained a fictitious value … immense nominal profits are made, but heavy losses counterbalance these and make the profits merely nominal. Bills [of credit] are as common here as peat dust is in the highlands.'
– NIEL BLACK'S DIARY, DECEMBER 1839

bamboozled into parting with their cash.

But in the early 1840s the supply of borrowed money dried up and land values plummeted. Many speculators faced ruin, including Farquhar McCrae. The house at La Rose was barely finished in February 1843 when bailiffs arrived to seize it along with his other property. A creditor even stopped McCrae's nephew on the road into town and took possession of his horse, forcing him to walk the rest of the way.

In the legal battles that followed, McCrae managed to hang on to La Rose, but he did so at his family's expense. He refused to repay a debt to his brother Andrew, who was also under financial pressure. Andrew was furious, and Farquhar fled to Sydney in disgrace. His estate was rented out, then sold to the tenants on his death in 1852. For more than 30 years it dropped off the speculators' radar. Through the gold-rush era and the long wool boom that followed, La Rose remained simply a farm. The money that flowed into Melbourne, making it one of the wealthiest cities in the world, went to other parts of town.

The suburban perimeter was rapidly pushed out as Melbourne's population grew. By the early 1840s the town had its first suburb in what was called Newtown (later Fitzroy), where Brunswick Street was lined with expansive bungalows nestling among giant gums. During the 1850s, these detached houses were replaced by terraces to accommodate a growing population. One of

MELBOURNE'S POPULATION:

Year	Population
1836	177*
1846	12,000
1854	76,600
1861	123,000
1871	191,000
1881	262,000
1891	473,000
1901	484,000
1911	586,000
1921	766,000
1933	992,000
1947	1,226,000
1954	1,524,000
1961	1,912,000
1971	2,579,000
1981	2,806,000
1991	3,157,000
2001	3,367,000
2006	3,744,000
2021	4,500,000 (projected)

Note: Indigenous people were excluded from the 1836 figure, and they were only counted consistently after 1971.

Sarah Bunbury painted this **watercolour of Brunswick Street** from the front of her house in June 1841

the largest and most distinctive terraces from that decade is Royal Terrace on Nicholson Street, Fitzroy, which had high walls of local bluestone above a single-storey veranda. But the houses of the gold-rush decade aren't always so easy to recognise, because many were given elaborate facelifts in the 1880s. My first temporary home in Melbourne was like that – a bluestone terrace built in the 1850s, it had been extended about 30 years later to include a two-storey balcony. The balcony kept the sun off, but was otherwise more decorative than functional; you could only reach it by ducking through the parlour window.

By the end of the gold-rush decade there were suburbs on both sides of the river, from Prahran, Toorak and South Yarra to Richmond, Collingwood and Fitzroy. Wealth in the embryonic city

The imposing bulk of **Royal Terrace on Nicholson Street, Fitzroy,** in 1864, and in 2008

Looking down the Yarra from Studley Park to East Collingwood in 1867, and 2008

St Kilda Road in 1864, and 2008

was largely a function of altitude: to escape the effects of primitive drainage and periodic floods, wealthy settlers sought out houses on high ground. There were especially sharp differences among the suburbs on each side of the Yarra, where the denizens of Toorak and South Yarra literally looked down on working-class Richmond and Collingwood.

Toorak, in particular, epitomised wealth and exclusiveness. The suburb took its name from Toorak House, an Italianate mansion completed in 1851 and leased as a temporary Government House for the next 25 years. With its large estates, private schools and proximity to town, Toorak was a magnet for landed wealth. The original holdings were discreetly subdivided into large blocks, many of which were taken up by squatters and financiers. As the wool boom wore on, their mansions became increasingly ostentatious in their display of wealth.

The shores of the bay had a different kind of attraction. From Melbourne's early years, well-to-do colonists had retreated there for respite from the dust and noise of town. Nineteenth-century mythology also emphasised the health-giving qualities of sea air. By the 1860s there was a commuter rush each evening as horse-drawn vehicles streamed across Princes Bridge into St Kilda Road. Separated by patches of forest and wetland, the bayside settlements extended far along the shore. Travel writer Isabella Bird, approaching the city by boat in 1874, saw 'villages of villas, half-hidden among the sombre-tinted woods … as far as the eye could reach'.

As the suburbs spread, the landscape was transformed beyond recognition. Where Caulfield is now, for example, was originally a heath with freshwater springs and waterholes between low, wooded ridges. In the 1840s it was mainly a watering place for drovers bringing cattle down from Gippsland. The land was surveyed in the early 1850s and sold in large blocks to squatters, well-to-do professionals and businesspeople from town. But it's hard to reconstruct any of this landscape from what you see today. Almost all the waterholes have vanished apart from Paddy's Swamp, which is now the lake in Caulfield Park, and the shadow of another wetland in the middle of Caulfield Racecourse; once a rough course over sandhills on public land, the racecourse had been formalised by 1879, when the first Caulfield Cup was run.

Even the estate houses built in Caulfield by the first generation of colonists have mostly been demolished to make way for suburban dwellings. One of the few still standing is Halstead on Bambra Road; it was built in 1857, but these days its main distinguishing feature is a three-storey tower added in the 1880s. Though Caulfield was linked to the city by train in 1879, most of its houses date to the early twentieth century, when for two decades it was Melbourne's fastest-growing suburb.

The divisions within the city were mirrored in its local government. Melbourne became a municipality in 1848, but six years later local government began to fragment, with a Select Committee recommending that a borough be formed for every locality containing more than 300 franchised householders. Within a year Richmond, South Melbourne and Collingwood had set up their own councils, and by the end of the decade, seven more municipalities had followed suit. Beyond the urban area, Roads Districts were established with elected boards, which became councils in their turn.

While the plethora of local governments left Melbourne's older suburbs with a remarkable legacy of grand municipal buildings, its effects were not all benign. The fragmentation helped to consolidate the inequalities of wealth between the suburbs on opposite sides of the Yarra. The northern and western municipalities, with their predominantly working-class populations, had trouble raising enough income to provide even basic services. Many saw their only salvation in encouraging new industries to keep their constituents in work and keep rate revenue coming in.

The main casualty was the environment, especially the waterways. Melbourne's noxious trades – the 'stinks', as they were

Above: And they're racing at Caulfield – VRC Spring Meeting, 1894
Below: The ball held to celebrate the opening of Fitzroy's new Town Hall in July 1874

called – mostly involved processing various parts of animals. Their output of effluent was horrific. By 1870, the slaughterhouses alone were dumping 4000 tonnes of blood and 35,000 tonnes of solids into the rivers each year. Tanneries, fellmongeries and wool-washes too used huge amounts of water and discharged it as stinking waste.

At first the 'stinks' were centred on the Yarra flats in Collingwood and Richmond, but in the 1860s Footscray began to court their custom. The municipality's hand was strengthened during the summer of 1869, when residents along the Yarra woke up to the nauseating smell of a river full of dead and dying fish. The Yarra had become so polluted that it no longer held enough oxygen for the fish to survive. A Royal Commission duly recommended that the noxious trades be moved downstream, and Footscray welcomed them with open arms.

But the advent of new industries did not solve the industrial suburbs' problems. Councils simply did not have the resources to provide roads and drains for their growing populations, let alone to dispose of their waste. The low-lying areas of Footscray regularly degenerated into bogs, and in winter the Brunswick newspapers ran weekly lists of mud-bound, impassable streets.

Waste disposal also became an intractable problem as the population grew. Suburban councils contracted 'nightmen' with horse-drawn carts to empty backyard privies, but

'[The Footscray councillors'] sense of smell has become less keen and two or three, I am told, have openly expressed their readiness to put up with any "little inconvenience" for the sake of a few pounds that would be added to the borough's revenue.'
– A CORRESPONDENT IN THE WILLIAMSTOWN CHRONICLE COMPLAINS OF FOOTSCRAY'S WILLINGNESS TO TAKE THE NOXIOUS TRADES, 16 APRIL 1870

*'There is not a tree, or
hedge, to relieve the
monotony of the scene.
It is water, bog, and
mud on this side, and
mud, bog, and water,
on that. Cows grazing
on the adjoining
meadows are knee-deep
in mud; men walking
along the undrained
tracks marked out
as roads are wading
through mud; and
every house that is not
environed by mud, is
surrounded by water,
which in the course
of a few days will be
converted into mud.'*
– HENRY CORNISH
DESCRIBES
FOOTSCRAY
IN 1880

there was nowhere to dispose of the contents. The result was that nightmen often dumped their accumulated loads on vacant land or into the nearest river. (The Johnston Street bridge on the Yarra became a favourite drop-off spot.) Typhoid, diphtheria and other 'filth' diseases claimed an increasing toll of life in the 1880s. There could be little progress while responsibility for sanitation was divided between 20 local councils, who fretted about costs and bickered about handing over any of their powers to construct an underground system.

It required the intervention of the Victorian government to break the deadlock in 1890, placing water and sewerage in the hands of a new Melbourne and Metropolitan Board of Works. An intensive spate of construction followed; mains were built east and west of the river, joining at Spotswood, where a pumping station dispatched the waste to low-lying land west of the bay at Werribee. The first houses were connected within six years, and by 1907 the city had been sewered.

If fragmented local governments were incapable of providing citywide services, they made extraordinarily good nurseries for land speculation. Elected by property-owners and dependent on income from rates, they were natural targets for 'boosters' intent on inflating the value of suburban estates. When speculation again reached fever pitch in the 1880s, many of the most notorious boosters were protected by strong local support bases

Tommy Bent, master of parish-pump politics, at the height of his career

– James Munro in Prahran and South Yarra, James Mirams in Collingwood, and above all Thomas Bent, whose twin bases were the wealthy suburb of Brighton and the neighbouring semi-rural Moorabbin.

Bent began his political career on the Brighton and Moorabbin councils, then represented Brighton in the Legislative Assembly for most of the period from 1871 till his death in 1909. The son of an ex-convict turned market gardener, he was an unlikely MP for the silvertails of Brighton; he once joked that his family tree was a cabbage. He was often ridiculed for his Australian accent, which struck a discordant note in a parliament of English voices. But Tommy Bent had come to parliament with a plan.

From his experience in local politics, Bent realised there were votes to be won in persuading electors that they deserved a share of the public pie – and, in particular, a bigger share than the electors next door. This was the insight around which he built his political strategy. Alfred Deakin described him as 'the most brazen, untrustworthy intriguer' in Victorian politics.

A speculator who borrowed heavily to build his private fortune, Bent applied the same approach to public affairs. His masterpiece, if it can be called that, was a Railway Construction Act that proposed putting a railway through every Victorian electorate – all based on hopelessly optimistic estimates prepared by Bent himself. While the Act promised windfall profits for Bent and his allies, who'd purchased land near the projected lines, it also prevented his opponents from protesting for fear of raising their electors' ire.

Bent did not remain railways minister for long, but the events he set in motion had a profound influence on the shape of Melbourne. In 1884 his railway measures were consolidated into a piece of legislation that became known as the Octopus Act, which approved the building of almost 1900 kilometres of track to form 65 railway lines. The cost would be £44 million – equivalent to about $9 billion in 2008 terms – and most of the money would have to be borrowed.

After the Act was passed, government railway construction was increasingly based on the principle of 'build it and they will come'. At first the gamble worked; people were flooding to 'Marvellous Melbourne' and the increased population produced a building boom in turn. The brick-pits of Brunswick were busy, timber yards were thriving, and builders were running up houses as fast as they could. Subdivisions sprouted from Essendon, Coburg and Northcote through Kew and Hawthorn to Moorabbin and Bentleigh, named after Tommy Bent himself.

But the railway boom soon began to outrun itself. While

railways to Essendon, Coburg, Preston and Sandringham might pay their way, extensions to Broadmeadows, Somerton, Whittlesea and Frankston were a different matter. The most extravagant folly was the 30-kilometre Outer Circle line, which began at North Melbourne and eventually reached Oakleigh via Brunswick, Fairfield and Hartwell, with long stretches running through open paddocks owned (not coincidentally) by the land boomers in parliament. Trains took more than four hours to cover the route, and passengers simply didn't use it. Opened in 1890, the line closed three years later. Its only remaining traces are the Chandler Highway bridge, which was converted to road traffic about 1930, and a section of rail that now forms the Alamein line.

At the height of the railway madness in 1890, Bent chaired a parliamentary committee that approved another 7400 kilometres of track. Few of these lines were built; the financial climate had already begun to turn as British lenders became suspicious of Victoria's lavish public works and decided they had better things to do with their cash. When the supply of borrowed money dried up, public investment went rapidly into reverse and private spending followed.

The speculative mania of the land boom had drawn in many small investors. Builders, professionals and farmers, in particular, had sold land for subdivisions and then been induced to put their money into various land companies. The largest of these were called 'banks', and took savings on deposit. Few people were aware that these companies were being used to siphon off funds into risky investment schemes. But they were about to find out.

It was here that La Rose re-entered the picture. In the mid-1880s the land came into the hands of James Munro, a prominent land boomer who was premier of Victoria for a short and disgraceful period in 1890–92. How much Munro paid for the estate is unknown, but in 1886 he 'sold' it to his associate John Woods MLA for £28,000. The following year, Woods re-sold the land to Munro's Real Estate Bank for almost twice as much. Woods died soon afterwards, leaving his widow destitute; she later testified that he'd been acting as a dummy for Munro in this transaction, which was designed to milk the bank of funds.

The Real Estate Bank next subdivided the land, which it dubbed 'La Rose Park', and offered 537 allotments for sale through the real estate agency owned by Munro's son Donald and his partner W. L. Baillieu. The financial terms were generous – buyers were only asked to stump up 50 shillings, less than a week's pay for a skilled craftsman – and the sales pitch played on popular fear of disease, emphasising the subdivision's elevated site and healthy air. The firm even produced some bad poetry for the occasion.

> *From Eden of old the first lovers*
> *Were ejected for folly and sin;*
> *Here happy and prudent young couples*
> *An Eden more lasting may win.*
> *The terms are just simply astounding,*
> *Which Munro and Baillieu give;*
> *Then put down your fifty bright shillings,*
> *And go to La Rose Park and live.*
> – Munro & Baillieu's pitch for the La Rose estate, 1887

But nothing could induce buyers to take the bait. The subdivision was too far from transport, and the nearest railway station, Coburg, was several kilometres to the east. In 1888, the speculators tried another tack, floating a company with share capital of £64,000 to take the subdivision off its hands. This venture proved a disaster; the shareholders lost their money, and the land stubbornly refused to sell. As the list of bankruptcies mounted, the La Rose Land Company became synonymous with the worst excesses of the land boom.

When their ventures began to teeter, many of the boomers took advantage of a Victorian law allowing them to avoid the public stigma of bankruptcy by making secret arrangements with their creditors. In 1891 the parliament pushed through a Voluntary Liquidation

Act allowing companies – including banks and building societies – to do the same. The Real Estate Bank was among the first to take advantage of the new law. Between 1891 and 1893, about 450 Victorian companies were liquidated or quietly disappeared. Half were involved in land dealing and a quarter in finance.

Bank depositors took fright and began to withdraw their funds; in those days banks issued paper notes that could be redeemed in gold, but few had enough hard cash to meet the demand. The panic gradually spread from the boomers' institutions to the major banks. At the height of the crisis in April and May 1893, eleven banks closed their doors; two-thirds of all savings deposits were locked up, and about half the paper money in circulation became worthless.

The effects in Melbourne were catastrophic. People who'd borrowed to buy houses lost their jobs and couldn't keep up the repayments on their loans. Those who'd bought vacant land couldn't raise money to build on it. Even everyday transactions such as paying wages and buying food were disrupted. As employment collapsed, there was an exodus from the city. In the worst years, between 1892 and 1895, Melbourne lost 56,000 people. From Footscray to West Brunswick and Preston, new subdivisions were left empty or gap-toothed when struggling home-buyers walked away from their debts. The deserted houses were pulled down and used for firewood. By the end of the decade, Sydney had overtaken Melbourne as Australia's largest city; henceforward the 'Queen City of the South' had to play second fiddle to its rival in New South Wales.

The other day I traversed the whole La Rose estate, looking for traces of that ill-fated campaign to lure home-buyers in the 1880s. There was nothing. The only nineteenth-century house standing is La Rose itself. Even in the twentieth century, the estate was slow to fill. At the end of World War I, twelve hectares of land were compulsorily acquired for war service homes, which were built in the 1920s and 1930s. There were two more attempts at private subdivision in the 1920s, but they were bedevilled by delays in completing the West Coburg tramline, the only practicable public transport to town. About a hundred blocks remained unsold at the end of World War II, when the government used some as sites for Beaufort houses – prefabricated places made of metal pressed to look like weatherboards. The estate has the largest collection of these houses in Victoria, and they've worn remarkably well. The last blocks were filled in during the 1950s, when cars came into general use. Here, as in other parts of Melbourne, it took 70 years and a new form of transport to translate the boomers' vision into suburban reality.

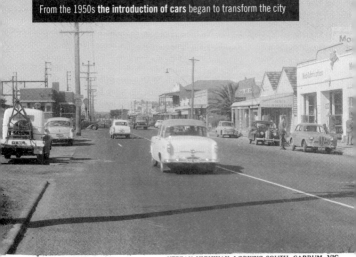

From the 1950s **the introduction of cars** began to transform the city

THE ROSE SERIES P. 2027   NEPEAN HIGHWAY, LOOKING SOUTH, CARRUM, VIC.

SIX

THE NEW ORDER

I've never forgotten my first visit to the State Library of Victoria's domed reading room. In those days, before it was restored, it was a gloomy cavern even in the early afternoon. The desks were long benches lit by green-shaded reading lamps. When I arrived, the place was full of high-school students whispering and flirting over their homework. One of the teenagers was someone I knew; I was looking for a book when he sidled up and asked me not to tell his parents I'd seen him there. Evidently the domed reading room was somewhere you went when you wagged school.

Once I'd found my book, I sat down and started taking notes, trying not to listen to the two girls next to me. Then one of them giggled, and I heard a loud 'Shhh'. I started and looked up. At the far end of the long bench was a raised station where a uniformed attendant was glaring at the teenagers, a finger to his lips.

I stood up to get a better look. It dawned on me then that the reading room was a panopticon – a surveillance machine. The long tables formed the spokes of a wheel centred on the attendant's station, which was elevated so that one person could watch the whole room without even having to stand up. I'd been reading Michel Foucault's *Discipline and Punish*, which has a lot to say about the panopticon as a technology of power, but this was the most elaborate one I'd seen.

Though the State Library's panopticon only opened in 1913, the idea went back to the late eighteenth century, when British reformers were pondering how to stabilise a society riven by industrialisation. The panopticon's aim was to make it easier to keep watch over people in the hope that they would become orderly, self-disciplined citizens. There were elements of this in the design of Melbourne's grid, which was intended to keep the public space in full view so that police could intervene at the first sign of trouble. But the unplanned emergence of the 'little' streets, where all kinds of activities flourished out of official sight, was a sign that the life of the town would resist being contained. This was part of the tug-of-war involved in Melbourne's transformation into a modern city.

From the first, the authorities were hard put to keep order in a town where so many people were constantly on the move. The pastoral industry employed a workforce of wanderers – shepherds, drovers and seasonal shearers. Many were ex-convicts, and the vast majority were men. When they came to town, they frequented taverns and 'houses of ill repute', where they drank hard and fought harder. Fistfights were the universal means of settling arguments; squatters and 'gentlemen' were no exception, though they occasionally duelled as well.

More serious crimes were shrouded in secrecy, especially where they involved violence against the land's traditional owners. Niel Black was keenly aware that he was entering a scene of bloodshed when he started looking for a pastoral run in 1839. There was a conspiracy of silence among the settlers, who would only speak in hints and riddles about events they would not name. Settlers were rarely tried for racial violence, and the courts refused to accept the evidence of Aboriginal witnesses, so the offenders went unpunished. In the case of lesser acts of violence, Kulin were reluctant to complain for fear that their attackers would be subjected to the cruel punishments the Europeans meted out.

Yet Indigenous people were often on the wrong end of the settlers' law. As Susanne Davies has observed, white murderers often had their sentences commuted, but Aboriginal murderers were invariably hanged. Melbourne's first hangings were of two Aboriginal Tasmanians known as Bob and Napoleon Jack, who had come with Chief Protector Robinson but escaped into the hills behind Dandenong and killed five settlers on nearby farms.

Under Lonsdale's command, police were given sweeping powers to regulate the streets of Melbourne. From 1838, they could challenge anyone found outside between sunset and 8 a.m. and arrest them if they couldn't give a 'satisfactory account' of why they were there. The same laws made it an offence for whites to be seen with Aboriginals without good reason. The maintenance of public order merged with the enforcement of a colour bar.

But in practice policing was erratic. It was hard to recruit police when there was so much better-paid work around, and many of those appointed were no better than the people they were supposed to pursue. Melbourne's first policeman, Henry Batman, was sacked for taking bribes, then lying to Lonsdale

'Endeavoured this day to get the white man who maltreated the black … punished. The Police Magistrate would not have anything to do with the case as it was aboriginal and the constable not exactly seeing the bludgeon fall on the black … Poor fellow, as we both came out of the Police Office, he says to me, "No wooglewoogle, white man only drunk." He was afraid we were going to hang the man.'
– William Thomas's diary, 18 July 1839

about what he'd done. Even Lonsdale's scourger, a convict called Henry Grimaldi, was punished for marrying without permission. The more Lonsdale tried to regulate everyday life in the town, requiring licences for everything from running a pub to operating a punt, the more he exposed the limitations of the forces available to him.

Port Phillip was under the command of the New South Wales governor until 1851, when the district was formally made a separate colony. Even then, citizens of Victoria had limited control over their own affairs. The governor appointed one-third of the members to the new Legislative Council, could veto or defer legislation, and still had exclusive control of revenue from the sale of land.

More to the point, while almost half the adult male population was entitled to vote, the odds were stacked against most of them. Fully 70 per cent of the population lived in towns or on farms, but they only elected eight of the 30 Council members. Ten were government appointees, and the rest came from the squatting districts. Historian Geoffrey Serle has described this arrangement as a parting present from the New South Wales Legislative Council, which regarded democracy as un-British. Sixteen more elected members were added in 1853, but the rural bias remained; nine of the new members were from the squatting districts and seven from the towns. Townspeople were in a permanent minority, with only fifteen members out of 46.

This was the body charged with formulating the Victorian constitution. The result was a parliament in which the Legislative Assembly, the popularly elected house, could not make laws without the consent of the Legislative Council, most of whose members were elected by rural property-owners. There were no provisions for breaking a deadlock between the houses. The power of rural interests was so deeply entrenched that in Serle's view, Victoria 'could never, throughout its first century, be properly described as a democratic state'.

The conservatives had gained control in the nick of time. Once the discovery of gold was reported, immigrants began pouring into Victoria. The population doubled in 1852 alone, and gold-seekers kept arriving in huge numbers for two years after that. Sailors deserted their ships, and labourers left their employers in the lurch. In England, convicts in the hulks at Woolwich mutinied, demanding unsuccessfully to be sent to Australia at once. The rushes seemed set to overturn the social order; an Anglican clergyman described them as 'the French Revolution without the guillotine'.

The track out of Melbourne and across the Keilor plain became a broad highway bearing a stream of men to the fields of Mount Alexander, Castlemaine and Bendigo. Rough-handed miners who had struck it lucky returned to town, where they splurged on wild binges in the theatres, brothels and bars; one pair of ex-convicts took only ten weeks to spend the proceeds of a £4150 nugget.

'Brawn and muscle are now the aristocracy, and insolently bear their newly-assumed honours. In fact, we have here the French Revolution without the guillotine.'
– REV. J. D. MEREWEATHER ON THE GOLD RUSHES, 1853

Diggers with handcarts, mules and horses cross the Keilor plain; engraved from a sketch made by J. A. Gilfillan in 1853

(That's about $8500 a week in today's values.) Townspeople who considered themselves better bred sniffed superciliously at the diggers' ostentatious displays.

But as the easily won surface gold ran out, diggers filtered back to the city, where they formed a shiftless and increasingly desperate underclass. For all the wealth washing through it, Melbourne during the gold years was a terrible place to be unemployed. Rents were high and food prices fluctuated wildly, as did the labour market, partly because public policies chopped and changed. At first, La Trobe used the income from gold to make patronage appointments, bloating the bureaucracy while spending little on facilities in town. When the press and the Council protested, he embarked on a spate of extravagant public construction. Then his successor, Charles Hotham, announced that the colony's finances were in crisis and suspended major projects, throwing many people out of work.

When the rushes began, the Legislative Council proposed tough new vagrancy laws allowing police to arrest people who lacked 'visible lawful means of support', whether they had committed an offence or not. The bill met furious opposition from the urban members of Council, led by John Fawkner, who desperately tried to delay it by making an interminable speech. When the exhausted members insisted he move a motion, he moved that the first word of the preamble be deleted and announced that he intended to do the same for every subsequent word. His tactics, however, could not stop the bill. In the eyes of the conservative majority, social order was more important than civil rights.

The policing of the goldfields was similarly high-handed. When the rush began, La Trobe introduced regulations requiring diggers to prove that they hadn't left their jobs without their employers' approval, and to pay 30 shillings for a monthly mining licence before they could start work. Protests immediately erupted, and the diggers refused to pay. Their civil disobedience exposed the weakness of La Trobe's position. He had only a handful of police, because so many had left for the goldfields. He urgently asked the British government to send troops from London. Four companies were soon on their way, along with 50 police volunteers and a naval man-o'-war.

But protests and civil disobedience continued. In September 1854 Governor Hotham became convinced that he needed to increase the colony's revenue fast, and ordered that the mines be searched twice a week to enforce the payment of fees. The goldfields were soon seething. At the beginning of December, some of the Ballarat miners took up arms and built a makeshift stockade at Eureka, swearing rebellion. Hotham sent all the available troops to the field, and early in the morning of Sunday 3 December, a force of about 400 stormed the stockade. Some 30 miners were killed, as were five police and soldiers. Soldiers ran amok, shooting innocent bystanders, bayoneting the wounded and setting fire to the tents where they lay. The next day, Hotham declared martial law.

News of this event travelled quickly to Melbourne, where the mayor called a public meeting to discuss what should be done to secure law and order. Several thousand people came, but the outcome was quite the opposite of what the mayor expected. Rather than expressing support for Hotham, speakers deplored the government's use of force and moved a resolution supporting the miners. Alarmed, the mayor tried to close the proceedings, but the meeting refused

A poster printed on 5 December 1854, two days after the Eureka rebellion; the public meeting that followed didn't turn out as the mayor intended

to disband. Under a new chair, it carried resolutions supporting the miners and calling for the dismissal of the Colonial Secretary.

Another meeting was held next day on the corner of Swanston and Flinders Streets. Again, passions ran strongly in the miners' favour. The editor of the fledgling *Age* newspaper suggested that the people might have no alternative but to rebel against the governor's tyranny. Fawkner jumped up and dissociated himself from any such conclusion, and others did the same. The meeting passed a resolution protesting at the governor's actions, then broke up peacefully. It was just as well; Hotham had more than 500 troops, jail warders and 'gentlemen volunteers' standing by in case of trouble.

From that point on, Hotham became increasingly isolated. He wrote to Britain asking for money to employ spies against 'secret societies' that were plotting his overthrow, and he refused representations to declare an amnesty for the Eureka rebels. When they eventually came to trial on treason charges, no jury would convict them. With calls for his impeachment on all sides, Hotham tendered his resignation in 1855, but fell ill and died before he could escape the colony.

J. D. Owens, a doctor who'd represented the miners in earlier negotiations, described the second protest meeting as 'the beginning of the history of the colony'. In some ways he was right. Revulsion at the use of force against the miners not only galvanised progressive

'At the present moment secret societies everywhere exist, but I have to trust to myself alone for the means of counteracting them … The French Red Republican, the German political metaphysician, the American Lone Star Member and the British Chartist here meet not to dig gold but to agitate, overturn the Government and seize the Land.'
– SIR CHARLES HOTHAM, JANUARY 1855

elements in Melbourne but also established the *Age* as their pre-eminent organ. Henceforward, it was in the paper's columns that they debated their visions of Melbourne as a modern city.

This emerging liberal establishment has been characterised as socially progressive and morally conservative. Its members favoured democratically elected parliaments and opposed the squatters' attempts to entrench their power in the Legislative Council. The liberal William Westgarth insisted the squatters were exclusives, not conservatives, because they were attempting 'to *rear up* institutions opposed to the people and the age'. Most of the progressives believed that all adult men should be entitled to vote and stand for election, and they devised a secret ballot to protect electors from bribery and intimidation. The elections held in 1856 under the new constitution were among the first in the world to use what became known as the Australian ballot.

It was a progressive article of faith that the inequalities of British society must not be re-created in Victoria. The democrats were mostly self-educated men of working-class or lower middle-class background, and they wanted to ensure that power and influence remained open to people like themselves. On every count, they ran into opposition from the squatting lobby; twice in ten years, during the late 1860s and again in the 1870s, there were constitutional crises when the Legislative Council rejected the budget and stopped the government's funds.

The progressives favoured reforming land policy to encourage small-scale farming so that industrious people could acquire a stake in the colony. Most wanted to support local manufacturing by applying tariffs to imported goods. They emphasised the civilising influence of institutions such as the university, the Public Library and the museum, which they hoped would make Melbourne the greatest and most enlightened metropolis in the Southern Hemisphere. Many opposed subsidising church schools, a policy that went back to Lonsdale's administration, and believed the state should offer secular public education instead.

At the same time, the progressives' vision was based on conservative ideas of morality, which they applied to society at large. Sober, industrious and respectable in their own lives, they attempted to devise institutions that would steer the wilder elements of society down the same path. Essentially, Melbourne's genteel reformers were trying to guide others towards their own particular idea about what kind of behaviour was normal, and systematic surveillance was the main weapon they used.

Prisons were among the first causes the reformers took up. By the mid-1850s Melbourne's prison population had far exceeded the capacity of the prison at Pentridge. Initially a wooden stockade designed to take the overflow from the city jail, Pentridge only had two communal huts, each holding 40 convicts. Once these filled up, prisoners were sent to Williamstown, where they were held in ships' hulks.

Between 1854 and 1857, John Price was in charge of Victoria's prisons and ruled them with a brutal hand. Prisoners were muzzled, strapped to their beds for weeks at a time, or tied, spread-eagled and on tiptoe, to bolts in the cell walls. Details of the horrendous conditions were aired in 1856, when some of the prisoners in the hulks were tried for murdering a guard during an attempted

Pentridge stockade c. 1849, painted by an unknown artist

William Champ, Melbourne's apostle of modern prison administration

escape. The *Age* publicised their evidence, and a citizens' committee pressed for an inquiry. The investigation was still underway when Price was beaten to death by a group of enraged convicts on the Williamstown foreshore.

His successor, William Champ, set out to create a professional prison administration and a system of enlightened discipline that he hoped would induce convicts to see the error of their ways. In the buildings of Pentridge, Champ's ideas took a dramatic and austere form. On his recommendation, the first stone building at Pentridge was a panopticon, with a central light-well surrounded by 176 single cells in three double-storey wings. The exercise yard too was partitioned into narrow wedges radiating from a sentry post.

Hooded prisoners being led from their cells at Pentridge, 1867

Once the permanent buildings were completed, Champ placed as many prisoners as possible in single cells with a minimum of furniture and no lighting. To promote rehabilitation, they were provided with uplifting books to read and prevented from communicating with each other. New prisoners spent up to nine months alone, speaking only to the warders and chaplains. They were made to wear canvas hoods whenever they left their cells so that other prisoners could not recognise them. After that, they were subjected to a regime of hard work, separation and silence in which their daily life was regimented by clocks and bells.

But for all the reformers' hopes, prisoners stubbornly refused to be rehabilitated. Once they had completed their sentences, they returned to their old networks of friends around the pubs and inner suburbs, and many were soon back in court. As an engine of punishment, Pentridge was diabolically efficient; as an agency of reformation, its effectiveness was nil.

Less obviously coercive agencies of discipline had far wider effect, and the provision of state schooling was high on the list. Even before the colony gained self-government, there was strong opposition to providing public subsidies for church schools. Reformers argued that the system was costly to run and left many children out. From the 1860s the government established state elementary schools and began applying common standards to the denominational schools.

Inspections revealed that many church schools were ill equipped to educate their students. In the fast-growing city, all kinds of buildings had been pressed into service. One inspector complained that churches were used without removing the pews, so that desks were placed 'exactly where they ought never to be allowed, i.e. round the sides of the room, so that every pupil may

Mass instruction in the schoolroom at the **Melbourne Orphan Asylum, 1874**

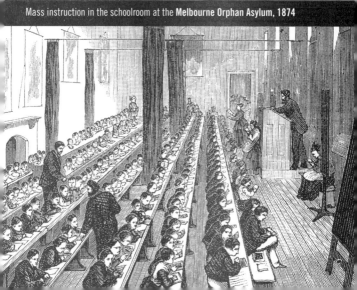

have his face to the wall and his back to the master'. Classes were large and unruly, and corporal punishment rife.

The Board of Education responded in 1866 by promoting a uniform classroom design. It published plans and supplied cheap materials for what was to become the standard nineteenth-century schoolroom: a near-perfect instrument of containment and surveillance, in which the teacher stood on a raised dais facing a bank of forms, behind which row upon row of hapless juveniles were temporarily imprisoned. The physical structure of the classroom implied a particular model of instruction. The teacher was set apart from and above the class, and the students were regimented into doing the same thing at the same time. Students learnt texts and tables by rote so that they could recite them for the benefit of visiting inspectors.

In 1872 the Victorian parliament passed an Education Act abolishing state aid to church schools and establishing a single centralised system of compulsory education. All children between the ages of six and fifteen were required to attend unless they had a reasonable excuse – mainly if they were attending a denominational school or could show they had already been educated to the 'required standard'. In practice, though, schooling was not as compulsory as it seemed at first sight. One of the commissioners at an 1877 inquiry into education acknowledged there was a covert policy of turning a blind eye to 'gutter

'I had no books and I couldn't read off anyone else's books … I think I taught myself to read – I certainly didn't learn it at school because I had nothing to learn by … I'd read a book a night by the candle – from the little Swan Street library up here. And I'd say the words over and over again until I could spell them.' – 'Jean Fowler' remembers teaching herself to read in Richmond

children' lest they 'impair the tone' of the schools. Besides, schools taught little more than reading, writing and arithmatic, so older children who could read and write were generally allowed to leave, especially if they had jobs to go to.

Working-class adolescents were often glad to escape the dreary and humiliating experience of school. Children from poorer families were taunted for their worn clothing and lack of books. As Pavla Miller has observed, though a significant number of working-class people became enthusiastic readers, their schooling did little to encourage their love of books. Progression from one grade to the next was not automatic, and many students were taught the same irrelevant 'facts' over and over again. At the turn of the century, only 20 per cent of the students in state elementary schools had progressed beyond Grade 4, and a mere 1 per cent had completed the Merit Certificate, which was awarded at the end of the eighth grade. Politicians and the public became increasingly disillusioned. In 1889 the age of compulsory schooling was dropped to thirteen as an economy measure, and during the depressed decade that followed, the state schools' funding was cut, programs curtailed and teachers retrenched.

The state system also had little to offer students who aspired to an academic education. When the Education Act was passed, private and denominational high schools had already been established in Melbourne's wealthy eastern suburbs, beginning in 1851 with the boys' school that became Scotch College. These schools enjoyed close relations with the university, which educated their matriculating students and supplied many of their teachers. The Act did nothing to challenge their monopoly of academic secondary education. The state had just a handful of 'central' schools, which offered a mix of academic, commercial and industrial studies up to the eighth grade; the city's first state high school didn't open until 1905, as a 'continuation school' to train junior teachers; it later became Melbourne High.

This first venture into state secondary education heralded

more ambitious reforms. The financial crises of the 1890s had eased, and there was mounting pressure to improve and extend the state school system. Much of the impetus came from the Director-General of Education, Frank Tate, who saw it as a matter of urgency that education should develop 'the highest and best of the native ability of the whole people'. He was supported by the new generation of liberals, including the politician Alfred Deakin and David Syme, proprietor of the *Age*, who believed that the state had a responsibility to remove impediments to individuals' moral and intellectual development.

In 1906 the minimum leaving age was raised back to fourteen, and in 1910 a new Education Act opened the way for the establishment of state secondary schools. It was some time, however, before the Act had any great effect in Melbourne. The Education Department was still unwilling to risk confrontation with the private schools; it focused its efforts on technical education for boys and domestic training for girls. In 1929, the city had only seven state high schools offering an academic curriculum. The suburban high schools were in Coburg, Essendon, Northcote, Williamstown and Mordialloc–Chelsea; University High in Carlton was used for teacher training, and Melbourne High had been relocated to a new brick complex in South Yarra, becoming the only state high school to encroach on the private schools' traditional catchment zone.

A second thrust of the 1910 Act was to tighten control over students' attendance. The old rule had required just four hours' instruction a day for 120 days a year, but the new Act raised this to 225 full days. A year later the Factories Act was amended to prevent employers from hiring boys under fourteen or girls under fifteen years of age. With rigid opening and closing hours, schools were at the forefront of the crusade to inculcate punctuality, not only on students but on the rest of the family as well.

As Alastair Davidson points out in his book *The Invisible State*, compulsory education opened the way for other forms of social regulation. This became especially tight under the 1910 Act. Teachers recorded daily attendance on a roll, and were obliged to inform a truancy officer if a child was attending erratically. The officer would investigate the family's circumstances, and if they were deemed unsatisfactory, the child could be declared a ward of the state.

These measures dovetailed into a de facto form of social welfare that was also a system of moral selection. In 1887 the Victorian parliament had passed a Neglected Children's Act under which private individuals could be licensed to remove children compulsorily from 'unfit' parents and take them under their guardianship. The new law was a boon to the well-bred female child-savers of organisations such as the Neglected Children's Aid Society.

A finely tuned moral calculus was applied to these children. Where a 'deserving' family had fallen on hard times, the Neglected Children's Department had long had a policy of allowing children to stay with their parents, who were given a small weekly sum of money to support the children through their school years. If this wasn't possible because a respectable parent was too poor or ill to support a child, a child-saver would assert her power as guardian and try to foster the child out, usually to a rural family.

But the approach to the non-respectable poor was far more punitive. Children of these families were generally placed in orphanages or in the prison-like industrial schools. The child-savers were particularly keen to keep children away from the rough subcultures that revolved around working-class pubs, which they frowned on as havens of drunkenness, sexual licence and crime. People who moved in these circles were regarded as shiftless and immoral; if they were poor, it was their own fault. In 1893 the Australasian Association for the Advancement of Science heard a charming paper from H. K. Rusden suggesting that such 'criminals, lunatics and idiots' be put down like dogs.

Rusden's suggested remedy was extreme, but many charitable

bodies shared his belief that the casual poor were an impediment to the progress of the human race. The same attitude could be found among the case-workers of the Charity Organisation Society, which co-ordinated the gathering of information about applicants for charitable relief. The society's aim was to ensure 'scientific' giving by making a detailed assessment of each case. Widows and deserted women were visited at home to make sure their houses were tidy, their children clean and their sexual behaviour chaste. Households where the breadwinner had been injured or become ill were subjected to similar scrutiny. Those who failed to conform on any of these counts were disqualified.

Many were rejected. Looking at the agency's case files from the 1920s and 1930s, Mark Peel found that charity workers responded more positively to 'respectable' applicants who felt the shame of their position than to rougher working-class types who appeared to feel entitled to charitable support. Peel has also looked at cases where the workers were led astray and found that in every instance the recipient was someone they had identified as a 'respectable' type.

What few of the moral improvers recognised was that the virtues they hoped to inculcate – sobriety, regularity, industriousness – depended on having a stable home and a reliable income that left something to spare. For many manual workers, this simply wasn't an option; casual labour was all that was on offer. Around the docks, in the building trades and in seasonal industries, workers were taken on and laid off from day to day or week to week. People who lived under these conditions had little time for cant about thrift and self-improvement. They had made a perfectly rational decision that it was better to enjoy life while they could and seek charity when they couldn't.

Equally, when moral reformers smiled on the respectable elements of the Melbourne working class, they tended to forget that these sober, industrious working men had achieved their regular pay and limited working hours partly through industrial action. In 1856 stonemasons working at the University of Melbourne led the building trades in a successful walkout that made them the first labourers in the world to achieve an eight-hour day. Workers in other industries went on to secure the 'boon', as it was known, and in 1873 a Factories Act applied it to women and young workers. The catch was that workers were often expected to do as much in eight hours as they had previously done in nine or ten.

Mechanisation also raised the pace and intensity of work. Half a century before Henry Ford claimed to have pioneered the production line, Victoria's light industries were organised on a similar system, with steam-powered machines setting the pace. At biscuit factories such as Guest's in North Melbourne or Swallow & Ariell in Port Melbourne, teenage workers placed dough on conveyor belts at one end of a travelling oven and packed the hot biscuits that emerged at the other end. In Collingwood, workers rushed back and forth to feed the huge power looms at Foy & Gibson's cavernous textile factory, which was part of a complex billed as the largest in the Southern Hemisphere. Along Gore Street in Fitzroy, the production lines at the 'Great White City' of MacPherson Robertson's confectionery works employed several thousand workers, most of them young women, making and packing sweets, chocolates and chewing gum. Work became an intensive activity performed between set hours, its pace regulated by the rhythm of the machine, and behind it the ticking of the clock.

To enforce increased work intensity, surveillance became part of the structure of the workplace. The messy, crowded workshops that characterised craft production gave way to larger buildings designed to speed the movement of goods, making it possible to break up complex tasks into smaller, repetitive jobs that workers could do with a minimum of training. Even small factories in the inner suburbs were arranged to make it easier to monitor employees' work. The supervisor or clerk would have a small office next to the entrance to handle orders and observe people's movements, while the boss worked upstairs in an office from which he could overlook the factory floor.

Shop assistants in department stores – or 'universal providers', as they were known – worked under similar surveillance, especially in matters of money. At Ball & Welch in Flinders Street or Foy & Gibson in Smith Street, Collingwood, the ceilings were crisscrossed by overhead wires leading from the counters to an accounts office with a view over the retail floor. When a customer paid for an item, the assistant put the money in a canister and sent it up the wire to the accounts clerk, who returned the receipt with the customer's change. This elaborate system prevented fraud and kept the assistants constantly under the clerk's eye.

Many of these places have now been demolished, and others have been refurbished beyond recognition. Last century's factories and universal providers have become this century's apartments and design studios, their saw-tooth roofs and tall façades the only sign of their original purpose. But what went on inside their walls inculcated a private discipline that was increasingly central to workers' sense of self-worth. More than all the reformers' efforts, it was the regular, intensive nature of this work – and the regular wages that went with it – that shaped Melbourne as a city of respectability and order.

SEVEN

A PERFECT BABEL

Yesterday I went to see an exhibition of embroidery and lace made by Italian women who'd migrated to Melbourne after World War II. The work didn't come from a public collection, but from the women's homes. Most of the fabrics had been woven from flax and silk the women's parents had grown, or from plants gathered in the forest and laboriously converted into thread. The embroidery and lace were exquisite, the fabrics fine and dense; you could tell that every piece was precious. Many had been made as gifts of love.

Several of the women were there to talk about what they'd done. One explained that she'd embroidered to ward off boredom when her husband went to work and left her in a place where no-one spoke her language. Others had worked in clothing factories and only had a chance to exercise their talents in their spare time. The beautiful things they'd made came from what they'd learnt in their home country, not from anything they'd learnt here. Outside their friends and family, they'd experienced Melbourne as a pretty unreceptive place.

In a city made up almost entirely of immigrants and their descendants, it's not surprising that differences between old and new arrivals have been a recurring source of tension. These differences were apparent from the settlement's earliest days. Though the colonists were predominantly British, the English, Scots and Irish brought long-standing prejudices with them. Convict transportation bore especially hard on the Irish. As a contemporary observer put it, people were 'banished from Scotland for a great crime, from England for a small one, and from Ireland, morally speaking, for no crime at all'.

Social distinctions were compounded by differences of religion. The Church of England's presence was relatively weak; there was a large Catholic contingent, and the Presbyterian and Methodist churches made their presence strongly felt, especially in promoting Sunday observance. The hawk-eyed members of the Lord's Day Observance Society helped to police the laws enforcing Sunday as a day of rest. They frowned on trading, drinking, socialising, playing sport – and increasingly on Irish Catholics who refused to toe the line.

If the local Protestant ascendancy was nervous about the Irish, the gold rushes sent them into paroxysms. About one in ten diggers came from outside Britain and Ireland. There were farmers from Ticino, an Italian-speaking canton of Switzerland, alongside contingents of Germans, French and Scandinavians displaced by the breakdown of peasant society in their home countries. American miners came from the Californian fields and young Chinese hopefuls from the Pearl River delta. Digging was a great leveller, making unskilled labourers of all alike.

The new arrivals changed the face of Melbourne. The city soon had fifteen foreign consulates, an all-American watering hole in the Criterion Hotel, a French coffee shop where people from the Continent could meet, and a precinct of Chinese eating-houses and shops in Little Bourke Street. The miner William Rayment described the gold-crazy city as 'truly a wonderful place … a perfect

ADULT EDUCATION IN VICTORIA.
THE ALUMNI PROCEEDING TO THEIR CLASS-ROOM.

A *Melbourne Punch* caricature of Melbourne's polyglot population in 1856

Babel' of languages and cultures.

But it's a mistake to exaggerate the diversity. Locals were usually first on the goldfields to take the easy pickings, and even the new arrivals were mostly British or colonial-born. The rewards of mining became erratic after the first flush, but landlords and merchants who'd been in Melbourne before the rush made fortunes through profiteering. In the words of Raffaello Carboni, the chronicler of Eureka, the fields became 'a Nugety Eldorado for the few, a ruinous field of hard labour

'The Chinese is jostled by the Russian. The polite Frenchman is abused by the African Negro … Men from all nations sit down at the same table and drink from the same bowl, they each talk and sing in their own tongue, get drunk according to their own peculiar fashion, quarrel, jangle, fight and embrace as their various natures dictate and … reel off to their respective beds.'
— WILLIAM RAYMENT ON GOLD-RUSH MELBOURNE

for many, a profound ditch of Perdition for Body and Soul to all'.

This was certainly the case for many Chinese. The first rush included several hundred Fukienese miners, some of whom made good finds at Mount Alexander. They returned to China about a year later, and their new wealth became the talk of the villages in Guangdong's Pearl River delta. Soon there was a rush to charter ships for the voyage south. More than 14,000 Chinese miners came to Victoria in 1854 and 1855 alone. About one-third paid their own way, and the rest borrowed money to finance their fares. The vast majority were from Guangdong, and almost all were young men.

Newcomers looked to their clan members for support. From the records of the See Yap society, Kathryn Cronin has estimated that just nine family groups accounted for half of Victoria's Chinese population. The clan societies greeted new arrivals at the wharf and found them accommodation. The societies had detailed rules governing everything from the miners' financial obligations to details of dress; for example, members were fined and physically punished if they went into the streets barefoot or bareheaded. The See Yap society reminded members of the need to 'gain the favour of the white men by quiet, orderly conduct' during what they hoped would be a short and profitable stay.

The Europeans showed no such forbearance. On the wharves Chinese immigrants

A view of **Little Bourke Street in 1863**, with Chinese residents in Western dress

often had to run the gauntlet of shouting, violent crowds, and on the goldfields they were repeatedly assaulted and driven off their claims. In the city, police harassed Chinese traders in Little Bourke Street and used the vagrancy laws to arrest anyone seen on the streets at night.

The Victorian parliament joined the fray. An inquiry into the goldfields recommended restricting Chinese immigration for fear that 'a handful of colonists may be buried in a countless throng of Chinamen'. (John Fawkner, who was a member of the inquiry, was especially one-eyed on the issue.) As a result, in 1855 an Act was passed restricting the number of Chinese each ship could carry and imposing a tax of £10 for each Chinese immigrant.

In the latter part of the decade, many Chinese were left destitute as the gold ran out. Some persisted on the goldfields, living in dwellings cobbled together from kerosene tins or anything else they could find, but many headed for Melbourne. Long lists of people seeking help to get home were posted up in Little Bourke Street, and many thousands of people returned to China.

As the population dwindled, people who had done specialised work within the community were thrown into the wider labour market, where prejudice excluded them from skilled jobs. European colonists also tried to enforce a sexual colour bar: young women suspected of consorting with Chinese men were arrested as vagrants and sent to reformatories, and some ministers of religion refused to marry Chinese and Europeans. The press ranted about

Illuminated arches and lanterns in Little Bourke Street celebrate **Prince Alfred's visit in 1867**

overcrowding in Little Bourke Street and the evils of opium dens – conveniently forgetting that the government had rejected Chinese pleas to have opium made illegal. In the face of this hostility, Melbourne's Chinese residents remained peaceful and patient, even putting up illuminated arches in 1867 to welcome the visiting Duke of Edinburgh.

In the 1880s further restrictive legislation barred Chinese immigrants from taking citizenship, dealing in gold or holding liquor licences. Furniture-makers were compelled to mark their products as being of Chinese manufacture, and were among the first targets of the 'anti-sweating' movement in the following decade. The tide of racist laws culminated in the White Australia Policy, the first substantive legislation passed after Federation in 1901. By that stage, Victoria's Chinese population had fallen to less than 7000 people from a peak of 25,000.

Until the end of World War II, Melbourne grew increasingly monocultural. At every census between 1881 and 1947, more than 95 per cent of Victoria's population were Australian or British-born. There was little tolerance of cultural difference; immigrants were expected to adopt the English language and Anglo-Australian customs. Wowsers frowned on what they called 'Continental Sundays', where social activities revolved around friends and family rather than church.

The 'British Type Best for Australia', the immigration propaganda proclaimed in the 1920s, but the problem was that fewer British types wanted to come. Would-be industrialists charged off to America, while those who aspired to an aristocratic lifestyle looked to the plantation economies of Kenya and Rhodesia. Living standards in Britain itself had also improved as the convulsions of industrialisation receded. People's friendship networks were in the cities at home, where they were increasingly inclined to stay put.

Besides, the news from the south was hardly encouraging. The depression of the 1890s had sent many immigrants scurrying home, bearing tales of hardship in Australia. Melbourne, in particular, no longer had the glamour that marked it as a starting point for intending settlers in the 1880s. Victoria lost population by emigration every year from 1891 to 1907, and the exodus had barely halted when the troops departed for World War I. A steady gain of immigrants in the 1920s was succeeded by another outflow during the 1930s depression. It seemed Melbourne was on the way to becoming an exclusive domain of the Australian-born.

The city did have an influential community of Jewish people from Britain, numbering about 5000 in 1900 and including several legislators and professionals of a liberal persuasion. Even the fragile tolerance they enjoyed was threatened in the 1890s, when a few Yiddish-speaking people arrived from Eastern Europe, and again in the 1930s, when the first refugees from Nazism began to come. At the outbreak of World War II, German Jewish refugees were classified as enemy aliens; their offers to enlist were refused, and some were interned.

But in one significant respect, interwar Melbourne was compelled to come to terms with cultural differences. From the late 1920s, Aboriginal people began to reassert their right to live in the city. Some came in search of work or big-city entertainment, others to escape the harshness of reserve managers at Cummeragunja on the Murray and Lake Tyers in Gippsland. They were joined by smaller numbers from Coranderrk in the north-east and Framlingham, near Warrnambool. By the 1930s Melbourne had about 200 Aboriginal residents, and 20 years later the numbers had more than doubled.

About half the city's Aboriginal population lived in Fitzroy, where Doug Nicholls played an important role in raising community consciousness. He was pastor of a Church of Christ chapel in Gore Street, and his persuasive preaching often centred on the theme that Aboriginal people had a future. He also had a high profile in the white community as a star player in Fitzroy's beloved Australian Rules football team.

Aboriginal organisations gained public attention with a Day

of Mourning in 1938 to mark the sesquicentenary of Australian settlement, and again during the 1951 centenary celebrations of Victorian separation. For the latter event, talent was rounded up from around the country to perform at a highly successful show called 'Out of the Dark, an Aboriginal Moomba'. Nicholls reflected afterwards that the event made Aboriginal audiences realise 'We should be proud of our Aboriginal culture – that we should remember we were a great people'. Though they continued to be targets of racial abuse – both verbal and physical – in the streets and lanes of Fitzroy, the Aboriginal return to Melbourne marked a victory over a policy of exclusion that had lasted almost a century.

World War II precipitated another major shift in official policy, though ironically it was sparked by the old racial fear of the 'Asian menace'. The setting was a world convulsed by war, and a settler society that for the first time faced a real possibility of invasion. The Japanese bombing of Darwin in February 1942 evoked white Australia's worst nightmare: an Asian attack across the thinly populated north. In the face of this threat, the Australian government decided to broaden its immigration policies.

The mass immigration that followed was closely managed to minimise cultural tensions. Arthur Calwell, the Minister for Immigration in the Chifley government, made sure that the first non-English-speaking immigrants were whiter than the average white Australian. Among the vast refugee population of Europe, he selected the fair-haired, blue-eyed people of the Baltic States as being most likely to 'fit in'.

Immigration officials heartlessly skimmed the cream from the refugee pool. They took the young, the fit and the strong, even if this meant breaking up families and leaving elderly parents to fend for themselves. Assisted passages were still preferentially offered to people from Britain. Over the period from 1947 to 1973, the government gave assistance to the vast majority of immigrants from Britain, but only to about one-third of Greeks and one-sixth of Italians.

Calwell also ensured that refugees got less than a free passage. Those who received migration assistance had to work for two years wherever the Australian government chose to send them. And, good Labor man that he was, Calwell negotiated agreements with trade unions and employers to ensure that displaced persons were offered only the least attractive jobs. While government propaganda promoted cultural tolerance, it was mostly the immigrants who were expected to be tolerant. Under the policy of assimilation, they were expected to remake themselves as 'New Australians', and those who took out citizenship were required to renounce their allegiance to their homelands.

Meanwhile, Melbourne's Old Australians freely paraded their prejudices in parliament and in print. The president of the Australian Natives Association referred to the refugees as 'European refuse', and the Returned Services League warned that Australia would be 'swamped by peoples of alien thought and dubious loyalty'. For decades, racism and xenophobia hid behind the claim that immigration threatened national unity. Some of the worst hostility was directed against immigrants with professional backgrounds; the Australian Medical Association, for example, flatly refused to recognise the qualifications of European doctors, in spite of the urgent need for their skills.

The refugees who came to Victoria in the ten years after the war arrived in the middle

'We must have a single culture. If migration implies multicultural activities within Australian society, then it was not the type Australia wanted. I am quite determined we should have a monoculture with everyone living in the same way, understanding each other and sharing the same aspirations. We do not want pluralism.'
– BILLIE SNEDDEN,
FEDERAL MINISTER
FOR IMMIGRATION,
1969

of a severe housing shortage. In 1945 there was a shortfall of 80,000 houses, and by 1951 it had reached 120,000. Australians and British immigrants were given preference in public housing, while European immigrants spent extended periods in hostels and 'transit' camps, where conditions were little better than in the refugee camps of Europe.

Once they had completed their mandatory period of contract labour and escaped the camps, immigrants generally went to the city, but accommodation in Melbourne remained tight. Everyone has a story about it – the Italian men who bunked three to a room in a Fitzroy boarding house; the Greek family of eleven who packed into a two-bedroom Brunswick bungalow; the Croatian couple with two children who lived in one room, sharing the kitchen and laundry with three other families on a roster system.

People from southern and eastern Europe could rarely get anything better than factory work; this came as a shock to those of middle-class backgrounds. Within the city, those who shared a common language clustered together for mutual support. Carlton, which already had an Italian community between the wars, became a first port of call for postwar arrivals, and Jewish refugees gathered around Princes Hill. By the mid-1950s many newcomers had gravitated towards the industrial suburbs of Melbourne's north and west – Broadmeadows, Coburg, Keilor, Sunshine and Footscray – where housing was cheap and their

'Apart from the language difficulty, we functioned. We shopped in Hungarian shops, read Hungarian newspapers, and felt at home with other Hungarians. We were both doing hard physical labour for the first time in our lives. My husband felt humiliated doing work he considered to be worthy of a junior apprentice … I felt no loss of status because I liked work and my colleagues. I consider myself, as before, middle class. But for the last three decades I know what it is to be a manual worker.'
– HUNGARIAN
    REFUGEE DUSI
    FABIAN

The Bissetto family's tailoring workshop in Bourke Street, 1947

communities were strong enough to form cultural, sporting and religious organisations.

Most people came as part of long migration chains. Often a man of working age would go first, then help other family members and neighbours to follow. Family ties and friendships eased the risk of leaving home, and co-operative efforts helped newcomers to establish themselves financially. As a result of hard work and sharing expenses, many were able to save for their own homes; by 1966, southern Europeans who'd been in Melbourne for five years or more were more likely to own a home than their counterparts among the Australian-born.

In the workplace, however, immigrants were concentrated in the hardest, dirtiest and least-skilled jobs. Many were prevented from working in their old occupations; as late as 1973, a government report showed that 23 per cent of family heads held jobs of lower status than they had in Europe. People who had arrived with little English found it an insurmountable barrier to promotion. Though other languages might be spoken on the shop floor, English was the language of management. It was also the language of education, medicine and the law. Only in the 1970s did policy-makers begin to realise how many of Melbourne's population were excluded from social services and civil rights because they spoke a different language.

Between 1945 and 1980 Victoria received about 1.7 million European immigrants, a third of those who came to Australia. Of these, 1.2 million stayed permanently, most of them in Melbourne. In regional Victoria the proportion of overseas-born people hovered around 11 per cent of the population between 1961 and 1981, while in Melbourne it rose from 23 per cent to 27 per cent over the same period.

The migration intake also became more diverse. In the 1960s the Australian government made assisted passages available to people from a wider range of European countries, and from 1966 it also began to relax the racial restrictions on immigration, letting in a small number of highly skilled people from Asian countries. Liberalisation continued under the Whitlam Labor government of 1972–75, which formally abolished the White Australia Policy along with a raft of other policies that discriminated on the basis of race. Multiculturalism was officially embraced at

'I went from doctor to doctor and none of them understood me. Where I went, they were all English. The specialist kept saying "Come back", and taking money … I could not make them understand what was needed.'
– A WOMAN EXPLAINS WHY SHE LEFT MELBOURNE FOR HER HOME IN ITALY

the instigation of Whitlam's flamboyant Minister for Immigration, Al Grassby, who presented a vision of a new, distinctive Australia that would be enriched by the contributions of many cultures. His powder-blue suits and yellow ties embodied the message: Australians didn't all have to look the same.

The changes in immigration policy didn't immediately take effect, because the government reduced the immigration intake during the period of stagnation that followed the oil price crisis of the mid-1970s. In Victoria, the effects of reduced migration were compounded by a manufacturing slowdown. For five consecutive years after 1975, Victoria lost people by migration to the northern states.

When the number of people coming to Melbourne began to edge back up again, a constellation of changes had occurred. Strife in Cambodia and the fall of Saigon in 1975 sent refugees fleeing from those countries. The civil war in Lebanon had a similar effect, though its impact on migration was smaller. Then, from the 1980s onwards, Melbourne received people escaping violence round the world: from Africa, from Central America, even from as close at hand as Fiji, where the 1987 coup put many Indo-Fijians to flight.

Differences of language and culture still translated into economic and social inequalities. Refugees, in particular, had great difficulty finding jobs. In the early 1990s these problems were sharpened by a recession that took a heavy toll on manufacturing and construction, both sectors that employed large numbers of immigrant workers. In 1993–94, the worst year of the recession, almost 30,000 people left Melbourne for other parts of Australia, and there was a sharp fall in overseas immigration. Unemployment peaked at 12 per cent, but it was far higher for many immigrants. Among people from the former Yugoslavia, for example, it was over 21 per cent, and among Vietnamese people a catastrophic 39 per cent.

The causes of these problems were deeply embedded in the structure of Melbourne's economic life. Many of the city's ageing factories had depended on trade barriers that were reduced or dismantled in the 1980s and early 1990s. In an increasingly deregulated economy, immigrants who'd been employed in those industries were in a precarious position. Textiles, clothing and footwear – all staple sources of employment for immigrant women – were particularly exposed to competition from imported goods.

In the late 1990s the city sprang back sharply from the downturn, but it did so by diversifying away from manufacturing. There was a flurry of growth in sectors based around new communication technologies, as well as in the older standbys of housing and construction. Now promoted as a tourist destination, Melbourne became a city of 'Major Events' and 'Major Projects'. Education too was big business; the number of overseas students in Australia increased ten times between 1985 and 2005, and about a quarter came to Melbourne.

At the 2006 census, Melbourne's overseas-born population topped a million for the first time. Many of the new arrivals were health professionals or highly skilled workers involved in the globalising sectors of finance, information and communications. Their impact was already apparent in the census occupational profiles: people born outside Australia were as likely to be managers or professionals as the Australian-born.

These changes are part of a global shift. Where earlier mass migrations in peacetime were mainly from declining rural areas, the people on the move now are more likely to be young, skilled city-dwellers. Some urban geographers have speculated that we're seeing a fundamental reorganisation of urban life. In US cities, for example, new-generation immigrants have formed residential enclaves dominated by people from their homelands, maintaining cultural separateness within an increasingly heterogeneous urban space.

But Melbourne doesn't seem to be going in that direction. It's not just the city as a whole that's culturally diverse but the individual suburbs as well. Three-quarters of Melburnians live in neighbourhoods with a significant number of people from different backgrounds. The most numerous exceptions are people of Australian or British birth, about a quarter of whom live in what geographers call citadels – areas where people of other cultures make up less than 20 per cent of the population. Outside these monocultural islands, the city has become a space that different people share.

The new wave of immigration has coincided with a long-awaited change in the shape of the inner city, which has finally broken the confines of the central grid. Beginning in the 1990s, red-brick factories on the south bank of the Yarra and derelict sheds at Victoria Dock gave way to office towers and apartment buildings. The new precincts have drawn a polyglot population of young professionals, international students and local empty-nesters who've decided to 'downsize'. After decades of what seemed to be terminal decline, the inner city has once again become a living place, and its tempo has perceptibly quickened. Once a byword for stuffiness, central Melbourne is now a province of the young.

EIGHT

THE REPRODUCTIVE CITY

When I moved to Melbourne in 1979, I was travelling against the traffic. The city was losing people to the northern states so fast that it was barely growing. My family, who are still up north, thought I was a bit mad. When you said you were moving to the city, Melbourne wasn't what you meant at all.

Slow growth had its compensations, though. I quickly came to love the texture of the place, with its brutalist blocks of Housing Commission flats interrupting landscapes of Victorian terraces, its nineteenth-century stone edifices squatting beside towers of glass in town. I came here for six weeks, and by the fourth week I'd decided to stay. I knew I'd found a city I could live in. More particularly, I knew it was somewhere I could consider having children.

There's a long history of romanticising the Australian countryside as a setting for family life, but it's at odds with people's practice. One of Melbourne's most obvious features is how quickly it became a place where women and children clustered. Migration separated women from their families and social networks, and they weren't inclined to repeat the process in Australia. The city's growth wasn't only driven by the rise of commerce and industry, but also by its emergence as a centre of reproduction.

A clear trend had emerged by 1861: while Victoria's rural population was about two-thirds male, Melbourne had almost as many women as men. And few generations in human history have produced so many children. The average couple marrying in the 1860s had seven children, who had almost as many in turn. The journalist Richard Twopeny complained that there was no escaping babies in Melbourne during the early 1880s 'unless you shut yourself up altogether'. Twenty years later, Melbourne had 41 per cent of the Victorian population and a majority were women.

It was a combination of choice and necessity that kept women in town. The city had a host of facilities the rural areas couldn't match. There were shops and delivery carts, schools, pharmacies, doctors and hospitals, and opportunities to visit friends. There were also more opportunities to earn money than in the countryside, where the only work available was domestic service. (The situation was even worse in the pastoral areas; most squatters referred to women and children as 'encumbrances' and gave preference to single men.) Melbourne's street directories list women as the owners of innumerable businesses run from home – taking in laundry, dressmaking, running small schools,

'Wherever his mother goes, baby is also taken. He fills railway-carriages and omnibuses, obstructs the pavement in perambulators, and is suckled ... in the Exhibition. There is no getting away from him, unless you shut yourself up altogether.'
– RICHARD TWOPENY COMPLAINS ABOUT MELBOURNE'S BABIES, 1883

The loneliness of the long-distance perambulator c. 1880, and **St Kilda Esplanade** again in 2008

teaching the piano, or operating boarding-houses and hotels. Even prostitution was largely a cottage industry run by women.

The nineteenth-century household was a hub of subsistence production as well. Even in the inner suburbs, back yards were turned into small farms, and livestock were grazed on common land. Most households kept poultry, some had pigs, and a few milked cows or goats. Growing vegetables and making jam, knitting and mending, making clothes and linen – all were part of the endless round of keeping house.

Women did this work in unimaginably difficult conditions. Over the gold-rush decade, Victoria added almost seven people to its population for each new house that was built; by 1861 the colony had an average of 1.4 people per room. To make matters worse, many of the houses had been thrown together in great haste. Roofs leaked, foundations shifted, and unlined walls let in draughts and vermin.

Even Melbourne's water was of doubtful quality. For most of the 1850s it was carted from the Yarra, which was increasingly polluted by the town's waste. One in five babies born in Melbourne during that decade died before they were a year old. The supply improved after 1857, when a reservoir was completed at Yan Yean on the Plenty River, but the lack of sewerage meant that 'filth' diseases continued to haunt the city.

Child-bearing and rearing dominated women's lives from their late teens or early twenties into their forties. Most felt powerless to prevent the endless succession of pregnancies. In England, women limited the size of their families by various methods – mainly withdrawal, abstinence or taking substances that produced early miscarriages – but Australian women don't seem to have known about these practices. Historian Marian Quartly has speculated that migration may have broken the chain through which this knowledge was passed on.

Women with large families were particularly exposed if their relationships failed or their husbands died. Men often walked out of their marriages; desertion was known as the 'poor man's divorce'. But a deserted wife had little means of redress. Even if she managed to locate her husband and get a court order for maintenance, he could evade the order by leaving Victoria. Once away, he could merge into the rural workforce, where everyone used nicknames and no-one asked questions.

Divorce was expensive, socially frowned on and especially difficult for women to obtain. Desertion alone wasn't sufficient reason; the woman had to prove cruelty or adultery as well, which wasn't easy if she had no idea where her husband had gone. As a result, she couldn't legally marry again unless she could prove her husband was dead. And otherwise there was a risk that he would come back and claim any assets she had scraped together – something he could do legally until 1884, when the law was changed so that a married woman's property didn't belong to her husband.

Widows and deserted wives received a small boarding-out allowance if they had school-age children, but otherwise they were dependent on charity and whatever they could earn themselves. But most were limited to occupations that were an extension of their domestic roles – making clothes and hats, cooking or waiting in hotels and eating-houses, washing and ironing, cleaning houses and offices – and for this work wages were far lower than in traditionally masculine jobs. Justice Higgins of the Arbitration Court laid out the rationale for this practice in the Harvester Judgment of 1907, and later in the fruit-pickers' case of 1912: men's wages should be based on the assumption that the worker had to support a wife and family, while wages in traditionally female occupations were based on the assumption that the employee had only herself to support.

The problem was that many women did have dependants – not only children, but siblings and elderly parents – and were doubly disadvantaged by the low pay and long hours involved in what was classed as 'women's work'. An inquiry in the mid-1870s found that waitresses and milliners were working far more than the prescribed

48 hours a week. In the hat-making season that led up to the Melbourne Cup, milliners were expected to work around the clock. Working hours were not as long for factory hands, but the pay was miserly. The working-class teenagers who made up much of the factory workforce generally earned between six and eighteen shillings (between $140 and $420 in 2008 terms) for a 48-hour week.

The issue of women's low wages was highlighted in 1882, when tailoresses employed at Beath, Schiess & Co., a clothing manufacturer in Flinders Lane, formed a trade union and went on strike to resist a pay cut. The *Age* condescended to back the 'helpless' women's cause and muster public support for the strikers. Caught in the act, the employers backed down, but from then on they shifted more and more work from the factories to unorganised outworkers, who had no industrial bargaining power. When the Victorian economy collapsed in the 1890s, outworkers' rates were cut below subsistence level and factory workers were sacked.

Unemployed women received almost no government relief. Men were offered manual labour on big public projects such as digging the sewer to Werribee and draining the Koo-wee-rup swamp. This established a floor under their wages: if an employer offered less than the relief rate, a man could refuse, knowing he could go on the public works payroll. Women had no such safety net. The most the government would do was lend them money

Young ladies training to be telegraphers at **the Technological Museum, 1872**

to buy sewing machines, increasing the competition for work and driving rates down still further.

But changes were beginning to occur in the workplace. Having already abandoned domestic service for work in factories and shops, from the 1870s women began to make their way into other occupations. Among them were teaching and nursing, the only professions girls could enter through work-based training after passing their Merit Certificates. Women also learnt to operate the high-technology equipment of the time: telegraph machines, telephone exchanges and typewriters. They were still far from receiving equal pay; state schoolteachers, in particular, took a hit during the 1890s, when married women were sacked and other women confined to poorly paid, dead-end positions. Nevertheless, it was clear that a growing number of women were reluctant to invest all their faith in marrying well.

In education too women had begun to look for wider opportunities. Girls' school attendance increased sharply after compulsory education was introduced, and in 1875 the Presbyterian Ladies College became the first private girls' school to offer a secondary education comparable with that of the elite boys' schools. The school's inaugural headmaster was Charles Pearson, an émigré from Oxford who had already emerged as one of the city's foremost liberal intellectuals. Conscious that academic study for girls was a novel idea, Pearson spent much of his opening address rebutting the charge that reading too many books would weaken girls' health.

In the suburbs, a multitude of small private schools opened to educate girls beyond the elementary level. By 1905, of 360 schools in the city and its suburbs, 152 were girls' schools. Though some mainly taught the accomplishments required for a young lady to make a good match, a significant number were run by professional women teachers and offered an academic program; some took students to matriculation standard. Meanwhile, liberals at the university had worn their opponents down in stages to secure the admission of women, beginning with the Arts faculty in 1879 and finishing with Medicine in 1887.

When people spoke of the 'woman question', though, they meant voting rights. A Women's Suffrage Society was formed in 1884 to press the issue, and three years later Melbourne gained a branch of the US-based Women's Christian Temperance Union. The WCTU viewed temperance as a question of preventing abusive behaviour by hard-drinking men, and was also active in promoting women's rights. As WCTU activist Bessie Harrison Lee put it, women had 'tried too long to fit their sons for the world; let them now fit the world for their sons'.

For years, women's suffrage was a fringe issue in the masculine world of politics. Among its few parliamentary supporters was Dr William Maloney, an early labour representative. As a child Maloney had shared his mother's struggles to support them both after his father left, and he became an advocate of women's causes. His first women's suffrage bill in 1889 lapsed without being debated; he had difficulty finding anyone to second it.

In the early 1890s Annette Bear-Crawford founded the United Council for Women's Suffrage to promote the issue outside parliament, with considerable success. The Assembly debated women's suffrage on eighteen separate occasions after 1894; it even passed several bills, only to have them rejected by the Legislative Council. The Victorian legislature became the last in Australia to concede women's suffrage. The conservative Council held out until 1908, and women only gained the right to stand for state parliament in 1923.

Meanwhile women's suffrage had been introduced for federal elections, along with the right to stand for parliament. Vida Goldstein, who had succeeded Bear-Crawford as leader of the radical wing of the feminist movement, stood for the Senate in 1903. It was the first time a woman had stood for election anywhere in the British Empire, and Goldstein gathered a respectable tally of more than 50,000 votes.

But it was William Maloney who became the first candidate elected to office by the women's vote. In a by-election in 1904, he won the seat of Melbourne. His supporters carried him on their shoulders through the city; they groaned at the *Argus* building and hooted at the Stock Exchange. Women employed in George's up-market store leaned out the windows and waved their handkerchiefs. The *Argus* raged that the representation of Melbourne was now in the hands of seamstresses, waitresses and prostitutes.

While the suffrage issue dragged on in the public sphere, a far deeper shift was taking place in women's private lives. The years from 1891 to 1911 saw a marked fall in the birth rate; the average family size fell to about four children. This precipitated a panic among those who believed that Australia must 'populate or perish'. Women were denounced for putting their own comfort above the interests of the race.

In reality, what was happening was more complex. At one level, the fall in the birth rate was a response to the 1890s depression, with its crushing unemployment and cuts in wages for unskilled workers. Many couples put off marriage and childbearing until times improved, and married couples became more inclined to limit the number of mouths they had to feed.

There was also better access to birth control information, with pamphlets on the subject widely distributed through feminist networks. The issue was publicly aired by many women activists, including Bessie Harrison Lee of the Women's Christian Temperance Union, who advocated chastity in marriage as a form of birth control. Marriage, she said, had been degraded into 'the most unholy gratification of man's worst desires', and the solution was for married women to say 'no' to sex.

A more outspoken advocate of contraception was the feminist Brettena Smyth, who supplied contraceptive devices and literature from her pharmacy in North Melbourne. Smyth explicitly described the use of various contraceptive techniques in her lectures for women at North Melbourne Town Hall. Her pamphlet *The Limitation of Offspring* outlined the dangers of excessive childbearing and argued that it was a woman's right to decide how many children she should have.

The tendency to limit the size of families was also related to the growing emphasis on formal schooling. It wasn't that women suddenly became literate (most already were), but rather that longer schooling increased the cost of supporting children, especially after the attendance rules were tightened in 1910. Families now had to support children until their mid-teens, when their food and clothing cost as much as an adult's. For working-class households, smaller families became a matter of survival.

At the same time, the home was more closely integrated into the market economy, becoming less a centre of production and more about consumption. The more commodities each household used, the higher the cash income it required, even with fewer children. The recovery after the 1890s was led by industries producing goods that had traditionally been made at home. Canned food became much cheaper with the mechanisation of can-making, and dairy companies and farmers' co-operatives supplied a wider range of milk products.

As houses were connected to gas, novel consumer durables entered the kitchen. Beginning in the 1920s, electrical appliance companies and the new State Electricity Commission mounted an unprecedented advertising blitz to persuade women they only needed to 'snap that switch' to brighten up their lives. New homes in Melbourne's suburbs were built with electrical wiring, and older houses were retrofitted. Electric power was still expensive, though, and was mainly used for lighting and smaller items such as fans and radios. Only the wealthy could afford the larger, more energy-intensive items; as late as 1955, one-third of Melbourne households had yet to buy an electric refrigerator and 60 per cent were without electric washing machines.

The first half of the twentieth century saw a boom in advice literature directed at women. Women's magazines such as *New Idea* and from 1933 the phenomenally successful *Australian Women's Weekly* carried an endless stream of information about cookery, health, nutrition and household management. Women were besieged by an army of experts who set out to inculcate habits of efficiency, thrift and orderliness. Their influence was also felt in the schools, which placed increasing emphasis on teaching girls 'domestic science'. Newspapers made space on their women's pages for an endless stream of 'handy hints' of the kind that Lennie Lower satirised in the *Women's Weekly*. ('Be sure to save the washing-up water for stock,' he gravely instructed his readers.) Daytime radio also addressed a female audience.

The aim of all this advice was not merely to make women thrifty, hard-working and efficient. It was also to turn the household into something resembling a business. Women were advised to maintain household accounts (though most didn't), to keep tabs on the energy value of foods, and to adopt a strict weekly schedule of tasks, with specific days for washing, ironing, mending, doing the silver and cleaning particular parts of the house. Experts also recommended that women schedule each day by drawing up a timetable and pinning it in a prominent place. Even babies were to be fed to a schedule, whether they were hungry or not.

Women were also responsible for their children's 'mental hygiene'. Children were to be encouraged in developmental play; they were to be watched closely, and each individual's needs were to be taken into account so that they would become clean, well-behaved individuals who could take their place in the adult world. This prescriptive vision of motherhood was a source of acute anxiety for many women with small means and small children, particularly if they did not have female friends and relatives near by to offer more down-to-earth advice.

The rationalisation of housework was accompanied by a segregation of work and leisure spaces within the house itself. The experts, joined from the 1920s by a chorus of architects, despised the old practice of eating and socialising in the kitchen. Eating was to be done in a separate dining room and socialising in the living room. Kitchens were to be treated as laboratories; they were to be small, streamlined and efficient, with no clutter to catch the dirt, and no table (though the housewife was permitted a solitary chair for her moments of rest). The working area of the house was to be hidden away, and with it the labour that went into feeding the family. For other family members, the home was a refuge from the workaday world; for women, it was an increasingly solitary workplace.

In 1929 town planners began moving to introduce a similar specialisation into the fabric of the city. Convinced that Melbourne's planning problems were those of 'Anytown, USA', they laid out a scheme that would designate distinct residential, commercial and industrial zones. In contrast to the nineteenth-century pattern where houses, shops and factories had grown up cheek-by-jowl, the new garden suburbs would be havens of peace far from factory sights and smells.

The first planning scheme was sidelined during the depression of the 1930s, which made the issue of urban growth irrelevant, but the idea of zoning was revived after World War II. In 1954 it was the organising principle behind a comprehensive blueprint for the city's future growth. Melbourne was to become an American-style city, with a sprawl of single-purpose spaces connected by road. But there were major flaws in the model. It assumed that everyone would have access to a car and that petrol would indefinitely continue to afford a cheap source of energy for transport. In the process, it radically widened the physical and psychological distance between work and home, public and private lives.

For all the propaganda about the virtues of homemaking as a career, women had been moving in the opposite direction for half a century by the end of World War II. The 1930s depression produced another drop in the birth rate, with the number of children falling to 2.1 per woman. At the same time, women continued to make up about a quarter of the paid workforce, in spite of resistance from government officials and trade unions. The main targets were married women, who were barred from teaching or working for the government.

The shortage of labour during World War II sent these policies into reverse. The marriage bar was lifted, and women flocked to support the war effort by filling jobs that servicemen had left behind. Women drove trucks, repaired aircraft and made weapons and ammunition; from 1941 they worked as conductors on Melbourne's trams. After much debate, women's wages were set on a sliding scale: they only received 60 per cent of the basic wage for traditional 'women's work', but rates were set much higher – at 90 per cent of the male rate, or even at equal pay – in jobs that were previously reserved for men. Women in these areas took home far more than they had earned before the war, but rationing and shortages left them little to spend it on. They put their money into savings, waiting for the war to end.

The peace brought a swift reaction. Women who had been doing 'men's work' were unceremoniously ejected in favour of returned servicemen. Patriotism muted their protests at this treatment, and the remaining 'women's work' held little appeal. In any case, thousands of couples had put off marrying and having children for the duration of the war; some had been waiting since the 1930s. And many now had saved enough to contemplate building homes of their own.

There was a marriage boom, followed by a baby boom. Suburbs encroached on the farms at the city's edge and filled in the interwar subdivisions. Public housing authorities were stretched to the limit trying to accommodate returned service personnel. As wartime shortages eased and new goods appeared in the shops, couples used their savings to furnish and equip their new electrified homes. Magazines, newspapers and radio were awash with advertising revenue, joined by television in 1956. Promotions for cereal, Vegemite and soap sang the same message: the ideal home was a site of consumption, revolving around Mother.

The shape of the house embodied this domestic ideal. Architects abandoned their crusade to segregate the kitchen from the wider life of the household, and do-it-yourself builders took matters into their own hands. The table came back into the kitchen, which was often located next to a room that combined the functions of an informal living area and a children's playroom (achieved in older houses by enclosing the back veranda).

From the early 1970s the walls between the kitchen and the informal living area came down. The kitchen was now set in one corner of a 'family room', a carefully designed panoptical structure in which women could keep an eye on the children (or the television) while they cooked. This had the further advantage of segregating the messier parts of the house from the dining and lounge rooms, which could be kept pristine for display. The bathroom and toilet were brought inside, giving the family room an uninterrupted view of the back yard as well.

Variations on this theme formed the building blocks for whole 'garden suburbs'. The catch was that these suburbs were too dispersed to support services within walking distance. Buses were the only forms of public transport, and they were rarely sighted outside peak periods. Without access to a car, the garden suburb was a trap.

Even the city's new universities reinforced the centrifugal tendency. Monash University opened in 1961 among the market gardens of Clayton, and La Trobe came six years later on a bushland site in Bundoora. Each was about 20 kilometres from the city centre, and neither was served by rail or tram.

Petrol-powered expansion also planted suburbs on some of the region's most fertile farmland. The fruit-growing area of Templestowe, 20 kilometres east of Melbourne, was essentially rural until the 1970s, when restrictions on subdivision were lifted after the government decided to construct a railway line to nearby Doncaster East. But the project was delayed by squabbles over the route, and its cost kept going up until eventually it was abandoned. Lacking the promised rail link, the suburb was built around the use of cars. Almost all the houses have at least two garages and some as many as five. Similarly Berwick, 45 kilometres south-east of Melbourne, remained a dairying village of less than a thousand people for 80 years after its rail line was opened, but rapidly turned

The rural village of **Templestowe, from the road** in 1898, and 2008

into a suburb when the freeway went in. The same story could be told all around the city.

The postwar suburbs, with their modern, owner-occupied houses, their cars and tribes of children, seemed to mark the triumph of the domestic ideal. Yet forces were already gathering to bring the ideal undone. The decade saw the beginning of a change in family life as dramatic as that of 1890–1910. For a start, couples again began having fewer children. The average family had 3.5 children in 1961, when the contraceptive pill appeared on the Australian market. Fifteen years later, the average was back to its 1930s level of 2.1, just enough for the population to replace itself, and it continued to fall from there.

These changes were part of a deeper shift that challenged the long-accepted division of labour within the family. Even in the 1950s, about one in ten married women was doing paid work. This increased to about 17 per cent in the early 1960s, when mothers of baby-boomers returned to work after their children reached school age. Then the number of married women working took off, reaching 32 per cent by 1971 and 56 per cent in 2004. Marriages also became increasingly unstable. By 2004, about a third of all marriages were ending in divorce, and married couples living together with children made up only 48 per cent of Melbourne households.

There's a certain continuity in these developments. As people live longer and families become smaller, physical reproduction has become less dominant in women's lives. At the same time, the broader social process of reproduction has become more demanding. Parents are now expected to support children into their late teens or twenties, and to expend an ever-larger proportion of their resources on the development of their young.

Once again, these social changes have left a legacy in bricks and mortar. In the dream homes constructed from the 1980s onwards, the collective space of the family room is supplemented by separate living spaces for parents and older children – the 'parents' retreat', the games room, and bedrooms with en-suites and independent access from outdoors. These houses are advertised as offering escape from marital and generational tensions: children can 'spend more time at home yet appear less often', and the segmentation of living spaces and bedrooms is such that parents too can choose to live (and sleep) independently under the same roof. That the process of acquiring these fragmented, privatised spaces is likely to fragment and privatise the lives of those who dwell in them seems, as ever, to be beside the point.

Main Street, Ascot Vale.

A postcard from turn-of-the-century **North West Melbourne**

IN THE 'BURBS

For most of this week I've been writing to the sound of piledrivers and backhoes. I live in the suburbs, but not that far out. It's a subdivision from the 1880s that only ever existed on paper because it depended on a tramline that was never built. The area went back to farmland until the end of World War II.

When places went up here after the war, none of them were very posh. The Maribyrnong explosives factory, which was still operating, used this side of the river as a testing ground. One of my neighbours grew up in the next street and remembers the rockets slamming into the hill at one o'clock every afternoon.

The Maribyrnong wasn't much of an asset, either. All kinds of industries – abattoirs, pipe-works, a paint factory – used it as a drain, and the tide carried their effluent upstream and down. Often the water stank, and sometimes it ran red. The river only began to improve in the 1970s, when the Environment Protection Act came in. Officially, the water is now classified as 'good', though no-one is game to swim there.

Like many postwar subdivisions, this one took a long time to build. The oldest houses are red-brick duplexes built for returned soldiers in the 1940s; our house, which is one of the later ones, was built in stages and eventually completed in 1961. When we moved here, there were still a few gaps where someone had bought two adjacent blocks as protection against a rainy day. (Having been brought up during the depression, that generation thought a lot about rainy days.)

As a result, there's a mix of building styles, from triple-fronted brick veneers to weatherboard cottages of all shapes and sizes. Some of the houses have gables; others are flat-roofed. I don't know of any that were architect-designed.

There's a reason for the visual mishmash. For more than a decade after the war, when it was hard to get labour and materials, one of the few ways of putting a roof over your head was to build it yourself. By the mid-1950s, about half the new houses in Melbourne were owner-built. An elderly man from around the corner once told me how he did it. Every weekend he'd leave his family in Port Melbourne and ride a pushbike up the river, pulling a trailer full of building materials. It took years to make the place habitable, and he kept working on it long after they moved in. There are a lot of houses like that around here – do-it-yourself places, some with obvious joins where rooms were tacked on as the family grew.

But by the standards of a later time, these houses were too small. They didn't have family rooms or en-suites, and their plans were often eccentric. When developers started eyeing the subdivision, they saw a lot of modest weatherboard houses sitting on relatively large blocks. Many of these places took years to build, but you can knock one down in a day.

The new houses that are replacing them are a mixed bag. There's mock Georgian, mock Victorian, mock Federation and mock Californian bungalow. Someone around the corner has gone for bluestone Gothic, and a few streets away there's a sandstone reproduction of a Regency manor house. Among them are a few flat-roofed modern boxes rendered in browns and greys.

Inside, though, they could be peas in a pod (apart from the sandstone manor, which has to be classed as a folly). Upstairs are a bathroom and three or four bedrooms, 'all with BIRs, master with en-suite', as the real-estate advertisements put it. Downstairs, starting at the front, are formal living and dining rooms (impressive but rarely used), a central bathroom, a laundry, and a family room with a kitchen in one corner, 'wonderfully appointed with granite benchtops and stainless steel appliances'. The family room opens on to a 'spacious private entertaining area' hard up against the back fence. If the site is large enough, there'll be parking for two cars on this level; if it's smaller, they'll be in a basement carpark. The whole thing isn't so much a home as a statement about affluence.

Variations on this theme are going up all through the middle suburbs. Politicians and planning authorities are desperate to make the city denser so that it can accommodate more people without choking the roads. They know the problem is urgent. Fifty years of road-dominated planning have turned Melbourne into a spaghetti junction of freeways and tollways, making it one of the most inefficient cities on the planet. In 2001, the last year for which I can find figures, there were 594 cars for every thousand people (children included), and transport accounted for almost 13 per cent of the city's economic activity. It's almost certainly got worse since then. The areas most affected are the outer suburbs, where thousands of low-income families are forced to own two cars because there's no other way to get around.

As oil prices rise, the postwar city is unravelling. People are scrambling back onto the railways wherever they can. Trains are running at capacity, which isn't surprising when you consider that most of the lines were built when the city was about one-seventh its present size. When you watch the 9.14 p.m. to Werribee leave North Melbourne – a sardine-tin of passengers, many with a 40-minute trip ahead – you can just about smell the desperation.

In principle, there's some clear thinking behind the latest

master plan. It's trying to marry the two main layers of Melbourne: the centralised city that developed around the railways in the first hundred years and the decentralised American-style city that spread out after that. The idea is to build up 'activity areas' around public transport nodes, and to encourage denser development in the surrounding suburbs so that people don't have so far to travel to work. The rhetoric is all about reinventing Melbourne as a sustainable city. But that's not what's happening.

The small developers who are setting the pace of suburban 'renewal' want to make money now. They're not interested in where the city will be a generation hence – in fact, they don't much care what will be happening next year. And right now, while energy is still relatively cheap, their safest bet is to build more of what the suburbs already have: three- or four-bedroom houses with plenty of space and ample undercover parking. Air-conditioning is a standard fixture too; around here on summer nights, the whole valley whispers and hums.

In the past few weeks, two houses on the other side of our street have been knocked down. If everything goes to plan, the new places will be finished by year end. Bricklayers are at work on one now, and bulldozers are excavating the other to provide underground parking for four cars.

Watching the big machines, I've been thinking about how much fossil fuel it

New houses on the Riverview estate beside the Maribyrnong River, with **Highpoint shopping centre** on the skyline

must take to replace a house, and how much waste it produces. Last week my neighbours' near-new timber kitchen was dropped into a dump-bin with a pile of broken concrete and hardwood floorboards, all bound for the tip.

I'm hoping our new neighbours will be people who care about the environment and take the bus to work, but frankly I doubt it. If they were, they'd buy something different, somewhere else.

The best chance is that they'll be people who work from home. It's probably the best chance for the city as well. In hindsight, Melbourne took a wrong turn when it set out to segregate the two – industry from garden suburb, public spaces dominated by men from private ones dominated by women. I sometimes smile to think of what Sands & McDougall would make of the place today. A listing for our street would show someone working from every second house. All the zoning in the world has failed to keep them apart.

From an unkempt village, Melbourne became an orderly, modern city, then a sprawling metropolis where everyone was on the move. Now it's part of a world of laptops and mobile phones, where value lies in information more than physical goods, and where people are connected in ways that make it unnecessary to rush around. It's already reinvented itself more than once. Now it needs to come to terms with another new order, or perhaps a new disorder.

NOTES ON SOURCES

1: KULIN COUNTRY

Photographs of silcrete quarry and Maribyrnong valley taken by the author.

On Melbourne's Aboriginal history, see Richard Broome, *Aboriginal Victorians* (Chatswood: Allen & Unwin, 2005) and Gary Presland, *The Land of the Kulin* (Ringwood: McPhee Gribble–Penguin, 1986) or the later edition, *Aboriginal Melbourne* (Ringwood: McPhee Gribble–Penguin, 1994). A recent discussion of the population issue can be found in Len Smith *et al*, 'Fractional identities: the political arithmetic of Aboriginal Victorians', *Journal of Interdisciplinary History*, 38, 4, 2008, pp. 533–51.

The Australian Project Gutenberg site has made digital versions of many exploration narratives available on the Web at <http://gutenberg.net.au/explorers-journals.html>. Extracts from Lieutenant Murray's diary are in Ida Lee (ed.), *The Logbooks of the 'Lady Nelson'* at <http://freeread.com.au/ebooks/e00066.html#ch06> and Matthew Flinders' *A Voyage to Terra Australis* is at

<http://freeread.com.au/ebooks/e00049.html>. James Tuckey's *An Account of a Voyage to Establish a Colony at Port Philip in Bass's Strait* can be found through Google Books at <http://books. google.com.au>. James Flemming's diary is in John Currey (ed.), *A Journal of Grimes' Survey: the 'Cumberland' in Port Phillip January– February 1803* (Melbourne: Banks Society, 2002). Richard Cotter has written an account of the abortive Sullivan Bay settlement in *No Place for a Colony* (Melbourne: Lacrimae Rerum, 2003), while John Currey has published *David Collins: A Life* (Carlton: Melbourne University Publishing, 2000) and an edited volume of Collins' despatches, *Account of a Voyage to Establish a Settlement in Bass's Straits* … (Melbourne: Colony Press, 1986).

2: Dispossession

On John Batman's life see C. P. Billot, *John Batman: the Story of John Batman and the Founding of Melbourne* (Melbourne: Hyland House, 1979); for a more critical view, see Alastair Campbell, *John Batman and the Aborigines* (Malmsbury: Kibble Books, 1987). Richard Broome discusses the 'treaty' in *Aboriginal Victorians*, pp. 10–12, and Penny van Toorn analyses it in 'Transactions on the borderlands of Aboriginal writing', *Social Semiotics*, vol. 11, no. 2, August 2001, pp. 209–27.

The State Library of Victoria's Port Phillip Papers Digitisation Project has made many of the early documents associated with the founding of Melbourne publicly available. Among them are Batman's 'treaty', which can be viewed at <http://www.slv.vic. gov.au/portphillip/0/0/0/doc/pp0007-001-0.shtml> and John Helder Wedge's field book, which is at <http://www.slv.vic.gov.au/ collections/treasures/jhw.html>.

Derrimut's story is drawn from Ian D. Clark, '"You have all this place, no good have children": Derrimut: traitor, saviour or a man of his people?', *Journal of the Royal Australian Historical Society*, vol. 91, part 2, pp. 107–32.

Quotations are from the following sources: John Wedge to

John Batman in Campbell, *John Batman and the Aborigines*, p. 131; William Thomas on the Melbourne Club in Michael Cannon (ed.), *Historical Records of Victoria, vol. 2B: Aborigines and Protectors* (Melbourne: Government of Victoria, 1982), p. 601; Fawkner on the reaction to the killing of Charles Franks in C. P. Billot (ed.), *Melbourne's Missing Chronicle, being the Jornal of Preparations for departure to and Proceedings at Port Philip* [sic] by John Pascoe Fawkner (Melbourne: Quartet, 1982); Sievwright's report quoted by William Thomas in his diary, April 1839 from *Historical Records of Victoria, vol. 2B*, p. 520; Parker from Mira Lakic and Rosemary Wrench (ed.), *Through their Eyes* (Melbourne: Museum of Victoria, 1994), p. 82.

3: Remaking the Landscape

Fawkner's diary is in C. P. Billot (ed.), *Melbourne's Missing Chronicle, being the Jornal of Preparations for departure to and Proceedings at Port Philip* [sic] *by John Pascoe Fawkner* (Melbourne: Quartet, 1982). Billot has also written a biography, *The Life and Times of John Pascoe Fawkner* (Melbourne: Hyland House, 1986), and Fawkner is the subject of a popular biography by Hugh Anderson, *Out of the Shadow* (Melbourne: Cheshire, 1962). His papers are held in the La Trobe Library.

The three-volume commemorative history *The Victorians* is useful on many aspects of Melbourne's history. The volumes are Richard Broom, *Arriving*, Tony Dingle, *Settling*, and Susan Priestley, *Making their Mark* (all Sydney: Fairfax, Syme & Weldon, 1984). The environmental consequences of European settlement are canvassed in William J. Lines, *Taming the Great South Land* (Sydney: Allen & Unwin, 1991).

On von Mueller, see Paul Fox, *Clearings: Six Colonial Gardeners and their Landscapes* (Carlton: Melbourne University Publishing, 2004) and 'Keeping aridity at bay: acclimatisation and settler imagination in nineteenth-century Australia', *Australian Humanities Review*, 36, July 2005, at <http://www.australianhumanitiesrevie

w.org/archive/Folder/03Fox.html>. See also A. M. Lucas, Sara Maroske and Andrew Brown-May, 'Bringing science to the public: Ferdinand von Mueller and botanical education in Victorian Victoria', *Annals of Science*, vol. 63, no. 1, January 2006, pp. 25–57.

Quotations are as follows: Lancey quoted in Billot, *Life and Times*, p. 107; Robertson in T. F. Bride (ed.), *Letters from Victorian Pioneers* (Melbourne: Government Printer, 1898), p. 34.

4: IN THE GRID

A readable and insightful history of Melbourne's early years is Robyn Annear's *Bearbrass: Imagining Early Melbourne* (Melbourne: Reed, 1995). On the grid as an imagined landscape, see Kathryn Ferguson, 'Imagining early Melbourne', *Postcolonial Text*, vol. 1, no. 1, 2004.

On the drownings in the streets, see W. Kelly, *Life in Victoria*, quoted in J. Grant and G. Serle, *The Melbourne Scene 1803–1956* (Carlton: Melbourne University Press, 1957), p. 98. On the lanes, see comments by Surveyor Perry in *Historical Records of Victoria, vol. 3: The Early Development of Melbourne* (Melbourne: Victorian Government Printer, 1984), pp. 219ff; on the growth of the lanes generally, see Weston Bate, *Essential but Unplanned: The Story of Melbourne's Lanes* (Melbourne: State Library of Victoria/City of Melbourne, 1994).

On public transport, see Robert Lee, *The Railways of Victoria, 1854–2004* (Carlton: Melbourne University Publishing, 2007) and for recent transport policy see Paul Mees, Public transport policy and land use in Melbourne and Toronto 1950 to 1990, PhD, University of Melbourne 1997, at <http://eprints.infodiv.unimelb. edu.au/archive/00000155/> (consulted 17 May 2008).

The Walking Melbourne website <http://www. walkingmelbourne.com/> is a mine of information about the architecture of many individual buildings. Rohan Storey has also published a book called *Walking Melbourne*, which gives information about 250 buildings in the central city area; it's available from bookshops or through the National Trust of Victoria.

The State Library of Victoria has assembled a website with links to resources on architecture at <http://www.slv.vic.gov.au/about/using/guides/resources/by_collection/architecture/arch1.html>.

Quotations are from William Thomas in *Historical Records of Victoria, vol. 2B*, pp. 532–33; 'Garryowen' [E. Finn], *The Chronicles of Early Melbourne* (Melbourne: Heritage Publications, 1976), p. 45 and G. G. McCrae in Grant and Serle, *The Melbourne Scene*, pp. 52–53.

5: A COLLECTION OF VILLAGES

'Looking west along Moreland Road from Glencairn Avenue in 1904'; image courtesy of the Coburg Historical Society.

On the history of Coburg generally, see Richard Broome, *Coburg: Between Two Creeks* (Melbourne: Lothian, 1987). Niel Black's impressions of the 1830s land boom are in Maggie MacKellar, *Strangers in a Foreign Land: the Journal of Niel Black and Other Voices from the Western District* (Carlton: The Miegunyah Press in association with the State Library of Victoria, 2008). Information about La Rose and Farquhar McCrae from Brenda Niall, *Georgiana* (Carlton: Melbourne University Press, 1994) and Michael Cannon, *The Land Boomers* (Melbourne: Melbourne University Press, 1986), which also gives an account of the scurrilous dealings associated with the land boom in the 1880s. A more scholarly account is Graeme Davison's *The Rise and Fall of Marvellous Melbourne* (Carlton: Melbourne University Press, 1979). Tony Dingle's *Settling* and Susan Priestley's *Making their Mark* outline the process of suburbanisation, as does Don Garden's *Victoria: A History* (Melbourne: Nelson, 1984). On Tommy Bent, see Margaret Glass, *Tommy Bent: Bent by Name, Bent by Nature* (Carlton: Melbourne University Press, 1993).

Laurie Burchell's very useful guide *Recognising House Styles, 1880s–2000s*, published by the Coburg Historical Society, is available from the society or through Information Victoria.

Heritage Victoria also has an abbreviated guide to housing styles at <http://www.heritage.vic.gov.au/page.asp?ID=411#8>.

The Australian Heritage Council's site includes profiles of Melbourne houses written by people who've lived in them at <http://www.environment.gov.au/heritage/ahc/publications/commission/books/ourhouse/vic.html>.

Quotation from Niel Black is in MacKellar, *Strangers in a Foreign Land*, pp. 89–90; the *Williamstown Chronicle* and Cornish's description of Footscray are in John Lack, *A History of Footscray* (Melbourne: Hargreen, 1991), pp. 91 and 88; Munro & Baillieu's bad poetry is quoted in Broome, *Coburg: Between Two Creeks*, p. 144.

6: THE NEW ORDER

Michel Foucault, *Discipline and Punish: the Birth of the Prison* (London: Penguin, 1991). Alastair Davidson has suggested an interpretation of Australian history drawing on Foucault in *The Invisible State* (Melbourne: Cambridge University Press, 1991). Martin Sullivan's *Men and Women of Port Phillip* (Sydney: Hale & Iremonger, 1986) discusses the process of class formation in the early colony, and Geoffrey Serle's *The Golden Age: A History of the Colony of Victoria 1851–1861* (Carlton: Melbourne University Press, 1963) gives a detailed account of Melbourne during the gold rushes.

On vagrancy, see Susanne Davies, 'Ragged, dirty ... infamous and obscene: the "vagrant" in late-nineteenth-century Melbourne', in David Phillips and Susanne Davies (eds), *A Nation of Rogues?* (Carlton: Melbourne University Press, 1994) and Lynette Finch, 'On the streets: working class youth culture in the nineteenth century', in Rob White (ed.), *Youth Subcultures: Theory, History and the Australian Experience* (Hobart: National Clearinghouse for Youth Studies, 1993). On working-class subcultures generally, see Graeme Davison, *et al.* (eds), *The Outcasts of Melbourne* (Sydney: Allen & Unwin, 1985) and Jon Stratton, *The Young Ones: Working-class Culture, Consumption and the Category of Youth* (Perth: Black

Swan Press, 1992).

Richard Broome discusses the changes in Pentridge in *Coburg: Between Two Creeks*, and Lynne Strahan looks at Price's rule in her history of Williamstown, *At the Edge of the Centre* (Melbourne: Hargreen, 1994), pp. 32ff. On the State Library, see Paul Fox, 'The State Library of Victoria: science and civilisation', *Transition*, spring 1988.

On school attendance and policies, see L. J. Blake (ed.), *Vision and Realisation: A Centenary History of Education in Victoria* (Melbourne: Education Department, 1973), vol. 1, esp. pp. 64ff; on secondary schooling, see David McCallum, *The Social Production of Merit: Education, Psychology, and Politics in Australia* (Deakin University Studies in Education no. 7, London: Palmer Press, 1990). Pavla Miller's comment is from *Transformations of Patriarchy in the West, 1500–1900* (Bloomington: Indiana University Press, 1998), p. 228.

For a portrait of a prominent child-saver, see Shurlee Swain's essay on Selina Sutherland in Marilyn Lake and Farley Kelly (eds), *Double Time: Women in Victoria – 150 Years* (Ringwood: Penguin, 1985), pp. 109–15. On the Charity Organisation Society, see Mark Peel, 'Charity, casework and the dramas of class in Melbourne, 1920–1940: "Feeling your position"', *History Australia*, vol. 2, no. 3, 2005.

Two of the best studies of respectability in Melbourne's working-class communities are Janet McCalman's *Struggletown: Public and Private Life in Richmond, 1900–1965* (Carlton: Melbourne University Press, 1984) and John Lack's *A History of Footscray*. On changing regimes of time, see Graeme Davison's *The Unforgiving Minute: How Australia Learned to Tell the Time* (Melbourne: Oxford University Press, 1993).

Quotations are as follows: Mereweather and Hotham in Serle, *The Golden Age*, pp. 30 and 173; 'Jean Fowler' interview in McCalman, *Struggletown*, p. 83; Rusden in Susanne Davies, 'Vagrancy and the Victorians: the social construction of the vagrant in Melbourne,

7: A PERFECT BABEL

Richard Broome's *Arriving* is a mine of information on Victorian migration through all its phases to the mid-1980s. The comment about the English, Scots and Irish is by Alexander Marjoribanks, quoted in Stephen Nicholas and Nicholas Shergold, 'Convicts as migrants', in Stephen Nicholas (ed.), *Convict Workers: Reinterpreting Australia's Past* (Melbourne: Cambridge University Press, 1988), p. 47. On the gold rushes, see Serle, *The Golden Age*; the comment by Carboni is on p. 163.

On Chinese migration, see Kathryn Cronin, *Colonial Casualties: Chinese in Early Victoria* (Carlton: Melbourne University Press, 1982) and Eric Rolls, *Sojourners: Flowers and the Wide Sea* (St Lucia: University of Queensland Press, 1992). Graeme Davison reminds us of the wowsers' objections to Continental Sundays in 'The European city in Australia', *Journal of Urban History*, 27, pp. 779–93 (reference p. 781). Richard Broome's *Aboriginal Victorians* discusses the Aboriginal return to Melbourne in chapter 14.

Postwar migration is discussed extensively in Broome, *Arriving*; the racist quotes are on pp. 177 and 179. See also James Jupp, *From White Australia to Woomera: the Story of Australian Immigration* (Port Melbourne: Cambridge University Press, 2007) and Andrew Markus, 'Everybody become a job', in Verity Burgmann and Jenny Lee (eds), *A Most Valuable Acquisition* (McPhee Gribble–Penguin, Melbourne, 1988). On the discrimination against doctors, see Egon Kunz, *Displaced Persons: Calwell's New Australians* (Canberra: ANU Press, 1988), pp. 190–92, and on the immigrant camps, especially Bonegilla, see Glenda Sluga, 'Dis/Placed', in *Meanjin*, 49, 1, 1989.

Quotations are as follows: William Rayment's diary quoted in Serle, *The Golden Age*, p. 68; Fauchery's *Lettres d'un mineur* from Tim Flannery, *The Birth of Melbourne* (Melbourne: Text, 2002), p. 182; Billie Snedden from Robyn Hartley and Peter McDonald, 'The many faces of families: diversity among Australian families and its implications', *Family Matters*, 37, April 1994, pp. 6–12; Dusi Fabian from Sue Fabian, 'Dusi Fabian: Hungarian refugee', in Lake and Kelly (eds), *Double Time*, pp. 428, 430; the quotation from the anonymous Italian woman is from Stephanie Lindsay Thompson, *Australia through Italian Eyes* (Melbourne: Oxford University Press, 1980), p. 60.

8: THE REPRODUCTIVE CITY

Statistics are taken from *Victorian Year Books*, various years. On the history of women in Victoria, see Marilyn Lake and Farley Kelly, *Double Time*; other information from Patricia Grimshaw *et al.*, *Creating a Nation* (Ringwood: McPhee Gribble–Penguin, 1994); Verity Burgmann and Jenny Lee (eds), *Making a Life* and *Staining the Wattle* (Ringwood: McPhee Gribble–Penguin, 1988); Kerreen Reiger, *The Disenchantment of the Home: Modernizing the Australian Family 1880–1940* (Melbourne: Oxford University Press, 1985). Charles Fahey et al, 'The other side of "Marvellous Melbourne"', in Jane Beer et al., *Colonial Frontiers and Family Fortunes* (Parkville: University of Melbourne History Monograph Series, 1989).

On women's private schools, see Ailsa Zainu'ddin, '"The poor widow, the ignoramus and the humbug": an examination of rhetoric and reality in Victoria's 1905 Act for the registration of teachers and schools', in Alison Prentice and Marjorie Theobald (eds), *Women Who Taught: Perspectives on the History of Women and Teaching* (Toronto: University of Toronto Press, 1991), pp. 92–113.

On the suffrage campaigns, see Marian Sawer and Marian Simms, *A Woman's Place. Women and Politics in Australia* (Sydney: Allen & Unwin, 1993), and on Maloney's triumph see Frank Bongiorno, *The People's Party: Victorian Labor and the Radical Tradition 1875–1940* (Carlton: Melbourne University Press, 1995).

On daytime radio, see Lesley Johnson, *The Unseen Voice: Cultural Study of Early Australian Radio* (London: Routledge, 1988).

On interwar homes, see Tony Dingle, 'Electrifying the kitchen in interwar Victoria', *Journal of Australian Studies*, 57, June 1998, pp. 119–27. Zoning, see Robert Freestone and Max Grubb, 'The Melbourne Metropolitan Town Planning Commission, 1922–30, *Journal of Australian Studies*, 57, June 1998, pp. 128–44.

On postwar developments see Graeme Davison, 'Images of modern Melbourne, 1945–1970', *Journal of Australian Studies*, 57, June 1998, pp. 145–161; Sarah Ferber *et al.* (eds), *Beasts of Suburbia: Reinterpreting Cultures in Australian Suburbs* (Carlton: Melbourne University Press, 1994), especially Margo Huxley, 'Planning as a framework of power', Kim Dovey, 'Dreams on display' and Tony Birch, 'The battle for spatial control in Fitzroy'.

Quotations are from Richard Twopeny, *Town Life in Australia* (Ringwood: Penguin, 1976; first published London, 1883), pp. 82–83; Patricia Grimshaw et al., (eds), *Freedom Bound I: Documents on Women in Colonial Australia* (St Leonards: Allen & Unwin, 1995), pp. 113, 156; Dingle, 'Electrifying the kitchen'.

Epilogue: In the 'Burbs

Photograph of the Riverview estate taken by the author.

The early history of the subdivision is outlined in Grant Aldous, *The Stopover that Stayed* (Essendon: Essendon City Council, 1979). Tony Dingle discusses postwar owner-building in 'Self-help housing and co-operation in post-war Australia', *Housing Studies*, vol. 14, no. 3, 1999, pp. 341–54.

ABOUT THE AUTHOR

Jenny Lee came to Melbourne for a few weeks in 1979 and decided to stay. Since then, she has lived in five houses, raised two daughters and worked variously as an archivist, editor and university lecturer. She currently convenes the Publishing and Communications program at the University of Melbourne.

ARCADE
PUBLICATIONS

www.arcadepublications.com

MADAME BRUSSELS
L. M. Robinson

Madame Brussels tells the story of Melbourne's most infamous brothel keeper. L. M. Robinson eloquently evokes the decadence of the 1880s boom era and the moral pandemonium that gripped the city at the end of the nineteenth century.

E. W. COLE: CHASING THE RAINBOW
Lisa Lang

Lisa Lang introduces us to Melbourne's most eccentric entrepreneur. From humble beginnings selling cordial on the Victorian goldfields to creating the world's largest bookstore and the iconic *Cole's Funny Picture Book*, Cole's life is the story of a self-made man and visionary utopian.